T0113854

THE BIBLE -
PRACTICAL APPLICATIONS
FOR EVERYDAY LIFE

STANLEY H. KOSTER

WESTBOW
PRESS®
A DIVISION OF THOMAS NELSON
& ZONDERVAN

WestBow Press books may be ordered through booksellers or by contacting:

WestBow Press
A Division of Thomas Nelson & Zondervan
1663 Liberty Drive
Bloomington, IN 47403
www.westbowpress.com
844-714-3454

ISBN: 978-1-6642-8494-4 (sc)
ISBN: 978-1-6642-8495-1 (hc)
ISBN: 978-1-6642-8496-8 (e)

Library of Congress Control Number: 2022922280

Print information available on the last page.

WestBow Press rev. date: 12/01/2022

CONTENTS

PREFACE

Is the Bible relevant for us today? After all, it was written long ago when customs and political and social circumstances were different. Do the applications found in the Bible apply weakly or perhaps not at all? It is my experience and view that the Bible is as relevant today as when it was written. It applies to people equally well then and now. Although things have changed over many millennia, our basic human nature has not. People laugh, cry, think, plan, love, hope, and fear—then and now. It should not be surprising that we can read ancient writings with understanding and emotion and find deep meaning in them.

In this book, I have attempted to capture some of the many practical applications found in the Bible. For each of these, I researched the scripture passages that pertained to it, arranged them into logical groupings, and then added brief comments. These summaries show the extent to which the Bible provides guidance for everyday living and how relevant it is for us. I have referred to scripture alone rather than commentaries, books, or articles written about the Bible. It is important to examine scripture itself so that we hear God speaking to us through His Word. I have found that studying scripture passages and relying on the Holy Spirit for insight and understanding is the most rewarding approach. Nothing can surpass the insights we gain through the help of the Holy Spirit. In fact, without the Holy Spirit, we cannot grasp the full meaning or apply what we learn from the Bible.

There are many good translations of the Bible available, and I have chosen the English Standard Version (ESV) for the majority of scripture passages. Other translations were used where the meaning seemed to be conveyed more clearly. These are noted in parentheses.

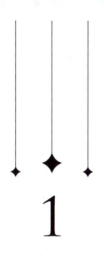

1

THE PRACTICAL BIBLE

All Scripture is breathed out by God and profitable for teaching,
for reproof, for correction, and for training in righteousness.
—2 Timothy 3:16

We all surround ourselves with things that are practical. We do seek out nonpractical things because they have some intrinsic or aesthetic value, but even these tend to be practical in some ways. Something is practical if it can be implemented, enjoyed, applied, or used to solve a problem; it is more than a concept, idea, or theory. We often associate the term *practical* with tools or things we use at home. For example, drinking glasses or eating utensils are practical because they assist in consuming liquid and food. But the concept of practical can extend far beyond physical things. It includes language, knowledge, information, advice, and so on. Almost anything that provides knowledge or skills can be practical because it helps us navigate through daily tasks, solve problems, communicate effectively, and accomplish work.

Perhaps you have never thought of the Bible as practical, but it is. It contains ancient history, stories, poetry and teachings, salvation, and the way to heaven, but it also has an abundance of practical applications to help us navigate successfully through life. And although it is an ancient document, the Bible remains as relevant today as it was when it was written. This is remarkable in view of the vast amount of change that has occurred since biblical times. Modes of transportation, construction materials and methods, agricultural techniques, and of course technology are a few of the examples of change. But there are things that have not changed; we are still human beings who talk, laugh, cry, eat, and sleep, just as humans did thousands of years ago. The Bible has remained relevant these millennia because the author is God Himself, who has a precise understanding of our human nature and foreknew all that has and will take place. He knows exactly who we are, what we are, and what we need. God provided a book like none other that is for all people for all time. As our creator, He made us in such a way that our basic human nature does not change, and thus all principles for living remain the same.

The Bible is authoritative like no other book because the author is God Himself. This is true because it contains the very words and wisdom of God. It was written by over forty authors in three languages (Hebrew, Aramaic, and Greek) over a period of about 1,500 years, and yet it is consistent and cohesive throughout. It is a one-threaded story about God's plan and purpose for us. This would not be possible were it not divinely guided and inspired. It has withstood the intense scrutiny of numerous scholars, archeologists, historians, and critics over many centuries. The overwhelming consensus is that the Bible is verifiable, historically accurate, and consistent from beginning to end. We can trust the Bible in its entirety.

Not only is the Bible true, but it is the one book that satisfies all of humankind for every circumstance for all time. It is a complete guide for life. As one would expect, it teaches us much about God, salvation, and life after death, and it provides answers to our most profound questions. But it also contains wisdom for everyday living that enables a solid foundation upon which we can build our lives and understand our world.

The Bible is read throughout the world in thousands of languages and continues to spread to the most remote people groups. One day, every people group in the entire world will be able to read the Bible in their heart language. Why has the Bible been read and studied among so many for so long? There are many reasons for this discussed below.

It is God-breathed (2 Timothy 3:16), meaning it contains the very wisdom of God, who inspired and directed each and every written word. The authors wrote down what God inspired them to say. When we read the Bible, we are literally reading words from God's own heart. This is important because God's wisdom is unsurpassed in this world. There is no authority above God and no true wisdom without God. Through the ages, women and men have desired to know God and seek His wisdom for living. Sadly, some have placed other books either alongside the Bible or even above the Bible. Even as there is but one God, there is but one authoritative book. The Bible stands alone as God's Word and is infallible.

The Bible provides answers to all of life's important questions, such as where did we come from, why are we here, why is there pain and suffering, what is the meaning of life, and what happens to us after we die. No other book answers these questions so clearly and completely. As we read and study the scriptures, each of the sixty-six books teaches us important truths. God is speaking directly to us through His Word and is teaching us, guiding us, and providing answers. What an awesome experience it is to hear God's voice through the Bible.

The Bible is so comprehensive and multifaceted that it is inexhaustible. No amount of reading and study can fully capture the content of its pages, nor can any individual or group fully comprehend all the truths it contains. Over the centuries, Bible scholars the world over have written a vast number of books, articles, and study guides in attempts to uncover the deep truths contained within scripture. Some have even written detailed commentaries in an attempt to explain the Bible in its entirety. But despite their thorough research and best efforts, they all fall well short. This is because the Bible has fresh meaning each time we read it and because the deeper we go into the scriptures, we find that there is still more to learn and apply. It is like exploring the universe; the farther into it we explore, we discover new things; there is always something beyond.

The Bible is a book we can read and study our entire lives, applicable to all age groups, from young children to centenarians. As we mature and our life situations change, we continually gain new insights. Men, women, teens, young children, and the elderly can learn and apply its content equally well. There are stories children love to hear and learn from, lessons for teens / young adults that help them learn and grow spiritually and navigate through difficult years, and life lessons that can be applied daily. It is a book for all adults, which enables them to learn new applications for family, friendship, and work/career situations through each season of life.

It enables us to cope with all of life's challenges. Even after a lifetime of intensive study of the scriptures, we can continue to uncover new meaning to ancient words. These can be used in new and refreshing ways.

Though it originated in a particular culture, it is a book for all people groups, cultures, tribes, and nations around the world. From the most remote parts of the earth to sprawling metropolises, the Bible is relevant to all. This should be expected because in reality, there is one human race of which God is the creator. All those who have ever lived are alive now, and those yet to be born are created in the image of God. Though our world experiences always change, the Bible can be read, understood, and applied wherever there are people.

The Bible is especially valuable and unique because it transforms. As we read the chapters and verses and study and absorb its truths, it changes us. The words have the ability to penetrate our hearts and minds and impart understanding—provided, of course, that we truly seek to understand it. This is accomplished through the Holy Spirit, who teaches and guides the reader. We begin to change inside, from the old self to the new self. Provided we read it with the help of the Holy Spirit, slowly but surely we transition into the likeness of Christ. We become different people, new creations as the Bible describes it; the old fade away, and we are transformed. This is a beautiful process, one I have personally experienced. Over time, it changed my thoughts, words, and actions. My desire for things of this world began to fade, and my desire to follow and serve Jesus increased. But the old self didn't let go easily, and progress seemed painfully slow. After many decades of Bible study, I realize that I still have far to go in my journey to be like Jesus. I have observed this same process in many others. Transformation goes beyond the individual; entire families, neighborhoods, communities, and beyond can be transformed. This, too, I have observed. Thus, the Bible is a book that induces measurable change for the better. This change has brought great joy to great numbers of people throughout the world. It is an experience like none other.

The Bible is of great help to us. It is a book that provides the knowledge, insight, and guidance for every aspect of life. No other book can begin to compare with the breadth and depth of the topics addressed therein. It provides guidance, answers, and hope for everyone for every circumstance or situation. Cultures and societies change over time, but the Bible remains just as relevant as when first written. It is a book for all people for all time.

There are many additional applications that could have been included in this book, but the ones represented here adequately illustrate the wide-ranging practical nature of the Bible. The others become clear through personal Bible study. As one reads and studies the scriptures, it becomes evident that the applications are endless. It is a book for all of life's circumstances.

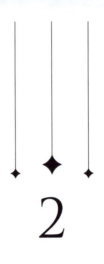

2

OUR RELATIONSHIP
WITH GOD

And the Scripture was fulfilled that says, "Abraham
believed God, and it was counted to him as
righteousness"—and he was called a friend of God.
—James 2:23

KNOWING GOD

We are limited in our ability to know and comprehend God. The prophet Isaiah stated this in Isaiah 55:8–9, where he wrote, "For my thoughts are not your thoughts, neither are your ways my ways, declares the Lord. For as the heavens are higher than the earth, so are my ways higher than your ways and my thoughts than your thoughts." There are natural limits to our ability to learn, reason, predict the future, and the like. Nor can we fully understand God's reasons for His actions. While our thoughts and ways cannot compare with those of God and our knowledge of Him is incomplete, we can relate to and know Him at some level. In fact, He desires that we know and relate to Him, inasmuch as he has revealed Himself. This enables us to fulfill our primary purpose—to love, worship, honor, and glorify God and have fellowship with Him. It is difficult to grasp the notion that the God of the universe knows each individual by name and desires to have a personal relationship with us, but it is true.

God has revealed Himself in two wonderful ways. First is His general revelation—creation. Genesis 1:1 says, "In the beginning God created the heavens and the earth." We can know something about God by observing what He has created, such as trees, birds, mammals, insects, water, stars, rocks, and the like. For anyone who believes there is a God, it is easy to appreciate His greatness, splendor, creativity, and beauty by what He has created. We can also know about God through His special revelation—the Bible. The Bible is God's Word. It reveals the heart of God—who He is and His desire for people. Every book, every chapter, and almost every verse in scripture teaches us something about God. We learn about Him by what the Bible teaches through its direct teaching about His character and nature, such as unchanging, all-knowing, holy, and sovereign. He has revealed Himself in the Bible by His attributes, character, special names, nature, and deeds. We also learn much about God through His names and attributes as described throughout the Bible.

What the Bible Teaches about God

There are hundreds of verses that describe God. Below is a sample that illustrates the ways that God has revealed Himself. God is all of the following:

Sovereign	Supreme ruler over the entire universe. Job 42:2 says, "I know that you can do all things, and that no purpose of yours can be thwarted." Jeremiah 32:17 says, "Ah, Sovereign LORD, you have made the heavens and the earth by your great power and outstretched arm. Nothing is too hard for you."
Omnipotent	All powerful; God is able to do whatever He chooses. Job 42:2 says, "I know that you can do all things, and that no purpose of yours can be thwarted." Genesis 18:14 says, "Is anything too hard for the LORD?"
Omniscient	All-knowing and complete.

	First John 3:20 says, "For whenever our heart condemns us, God is greater than our heart, and he knows everything."
Omnipresent	Present everywhere.
	Proverbs 15:3 says, "The eyes of the Lord are in every place."
	See Psalm 139:7–12.
Immutable	Never changing; the same before, now, forever.
	Malachi 3:6 says, "I am the Lord, I change not."
Eternal	No beginning or end; not bound by the dimension of time.
	Revelations 1:8 says, "I am the Alpha and the Omega, says the Lord God, who is, and who was, and who is to come, the Almighty."
Truth	Completely accurate, honest.
	Psalm 119:160 says, "The sum of your word is truth, and every one of your righteous rules endures forever."
Mighty	God's strength and power know no limits.
	Psalm 93:4 says, "The Lord on high is mighty."
Majestic	God is magnificent, clothed in royalty.
	Psalm 8:1 says, "How majestic is your name in all the earth."
	Psalm 93:1 says, "The Lord is robed in majesty.
Awesome	God is amazing, awe-inspiring.
	Deuteronomy 7:21 says, "A great and awesome God."
Great	God is above all people and things; He is incomparable.
	Psalm 145:3 says, "His greatness no one can fathom."
Holy	Set apart, perfect in every way.
	Isaiah 6:3 says, "Holy, Holy, Holy is the Lord almighty."
Righteous	God is morally right and just.
	Psalm 11:7 says, "For the Lord is righteous; he loves righteous deeds; the upright shall behold his face."
Love	The source of all love.

	First John 4:16 says, "God is love." Psalm 57:10 says, "For great is your love."
Faithful	God is always true to His Word.
	Psalm 119:90 says, "Your faithfulness endures to all generations."
Merciful	God is forgiving, compassionate, and gracious.
	Psalm 145:9 says, "The LORD is good to all, and his mercy is over all that he has made."
Compassionate	God has sympathy and concern.
	Matthew 9:6 says, "When he saw the crowds, he had compassion for them, because they were harassed and helpless, like sheep without a shepherd."
Faithful	God is completely faithful to his promises.
	Deuteronomy 32:4 says, "He is the Rock, his works are perfect, and all his ways are just. A faithful God who does no wrong, upright and just is he."

Some of the above items are unique to God, such as His omnipresence, omnipotence, omniscience, and eternal nature. But we also see others words that are familiar to us. For example, God loves, forgives, blesses, protects, listens, saves, imparts wisdom, and shows mercy. We also can perform all of these, though imperfectly, because we were designed to have some capacity to love, forgive, and the like. He is indeed someone with whom we can relate to and fellowship.

Though there is *one* God, the Bible teaches us that He exists in three distinct persons: the Father, the Son, and the Holy Spirit. God is triune, existing in perfect harmony. While this may be difficult to comprehend in human terms, it is a beautiful picture of perfect love, fellowship, and unity. It is what makes God so great. Each person plays a vitally important role in our salvation and spiritual development, all of which is clearly explained in the Bible.

God has revealed all that we need to know about Him to live fulfilled and meaningful lives. It is comforting to know that there is a God who loves us more than we can ever imagine and desires a relationship with us. One of the most profound truths in the Bible is that our great God and Savior went to the greatest lengths possible for our salvation. And all those who put their faith and trust in Jesus will have eternal live. This means that they will spend eternity with Him in heaven. And for our existence here on earth, God has provided all the practical things discussed in this book and more for our benefit—to enable us to succeed during our journey on this earth.

As previously mentioned, every book, chapter, and verse in the Bible teaches us something about God, and the above paragraphs are but a brief summary of what we know about Him.

God has also revealed much about Himself through His creation. As we observe and study plants, animals, cells, genetics, anatomy, physiology, elements, planets, and stars, we see evidence of His handiwork everywhere. Even the simplest organisms demonstrate amazing intricacies of life. The design of our earth, and indeed the entire universe, demonstrates God's handiwork. The vastness of the universe, stunning complexity of the biological world, and beauty and grandeur of the natural world are a reflection of God the creator. Too, consider the nature of human beings; our ability to communicate, love, worship, and create all exist because we were made that way. There really is a God; study the Bible, and His works will become real to you, as will the practical things He gave to us.

Through experience, I discovered that the more I learned about God, the more I came to appreciate the practical nature of the Bible. How then does knowing God help us practically? It helps in two ways. First, it helps us see that we have a forever friend, a best possible friend. Because God made us, He knows *everything* about us. He knows who we are and what we are He knows our skills, abilities, what we need, and, most importantly, what is best for us. Knowing that there is a loving, caring God who understands us completely provides the assurance that there is someone who will help us every step of the way. It is comforting to know that God has both the desire and ability to help us apply His special instructions for our lives. We are not expected to apply the Bible on our own, and, indeed, we cannot. God is the source of all knowledge and wisdom, and when we look to Him to help us, He will do so without hesitation. And He wants to be completely involved in our lives each step of the way. Second, knowing God is also practical because it helps us know and understand ourselves. We are made in God's image, and therefore we find our identity in Him. Just like knowing something about your ancestors helps explain why you think or act the way you do, knowing your creator helps you gain a perspective on you as a person. For example, none of us are omnipotent or omniscient, and we know that there are limits to our power and knowledge. Moreover, we all have weaknesses that limit us in many ways. Knowing this helps us see ourselves accurately and seek the help we need to navigate through life. One of the practical ways this is accomplished is through prayer.

HOW TO PRAY

Prayer is communication with God, and the Bible teaches us how to do it. God originated prayer to provide a means of approaching Him and intended that we do so regularly. God listens to us and then answers in His way and His time.

The Reasons for Prayer

We should pray because God wants us to. This is clear from the many scripture passages that affirm that God invites us to pray. In these invitations, God says three things to us: "I want you to pray, I will listen to you, and I will answer you." Isn't that amazing? The creator of the universe wants to communicate directly with us in a most intimate way—personal one-on-one conversation with the Almighty God. Consider the following passages:

> Then you will call upon me and come and pray to me, and I will hear you. (Jeremiah 29:12)

> Ask, and it will be given to you; seek, and you will find; knock, and it will be opened to you. (Matthew 7:7)

> If you abide in me, and my words abide in you, ask whatever you wish, and it will be done for you. (John 15:7)

> And this is the confidence that we have toward him, that
> if we ask anything according to his will he hears us. (1
> John 5:14)

The fact that God wants to communicate directly with us indicates how important we are to Him; we are created in His image, and we are special to Him in every way. He loves and cares for us more deeply than we know. Note that in the 1 John 5:14 passage, God invites us to come with confidence. This is because He will listen to each and every desire of our heart, no matter how great or small it is.

We pray to take away our fears and anxieties. God knows and completely understands that sometimes we are afraid and anxious about life. He wants us to take all of it to Him. Why? Because He cares for us and wants us to know that He is always there for us – to listen and to help. We are never alone. Note in the Philippians passage that it says *everything*. There is nothing off-limits with God, as we see in the following verses:

> Do not be anxious about anything, but in everything
> by prayer and supplication with thanksgiving let your
> requests be made known to God. (Philippians 4:6)

> Cast your burden on the LORD, and he will sustain you; he
> will never permit the righteous to be moved. (Psalm 55:22)

God is far bigger than any problem we might face on this earth, and He is capable of solving even the most impossible challenge.

We pray because God wants to help us and bless us. God knows our needs and desires good things for us. This is illustrated well by the prophet Jeremiah, who wrote "For I know the plans *I have for you*," declares the LORD, "plans to prosper you and not to harm you, plans to give you hope and a future" (Jeremiah 29:11). These words were spoken to the prophet Jeremiah during the exile of the Jewish people. They went through an extremely difficult time, but God saw the future, and His plans will prevail. In 1 John 3:22, we read, "And whatever we ask we receive from him, because we keep his commandments and do what pleases him." And in Psalm 145:18, it says "The Lord is near to all who call on him, to all who call on him in truth." And finally, the prophet Jeremiah wrote, "Call to me and I will answer you, and will tell you great and hidden things that you have not known" (Jeremiah33:3).

We pray because God wants to forgive us. Everyone sins and is in need of God's forgiveness. Second Chronicles 7:14 states, "If my people who are called by my name humble themselves, and pray and seek my face and turn from their wicked ways, then I will hear from heaven and will forgive their sin and heal their land." And in 1 John 1:9, it says, "If we confess our sins He is faithful and just and will forgive us our sins and purify us from all unrighteousness." God wants us to acknowledge what we have done wrong and ask for His forgiveness. This is one of His ways of helping us overcome our shortcomings and to grow in our faith.

We pray to deliver us from our problems. In James 5:13, we find "Is anyone among you suffering? Let him pray." Jesus understands suffering and invites us to bring our troubles to Him. And in Psalm 18:6, the psalmist wrote, "In my distress I called upon the Lord; to my God I cried for help. From his temple he heard my voice, and my cry to him reached his ears." And in Psalm 34:17, it says, "When the righteous cry for help, the Lord hears and delivers them out of all their troubles."

We pray so that we can resist temptation. Matthew 26:41 says, "Watch and pray that you may not enter into temptation. The spirit indeed is willing, but the flesh is weak." Through prayer, we gain the strength to resist any type of temptation that we might face. Temptation is all around us each day, but with God's help, we can resist and overcome all kinds of temptations.

The bottom line is that God takes prayer very seriously, and therefore we must too. In the section below are biblical guidelines that help us pray effectively.

Guidelines for Prayer

There are many Bible passages that provide a guide for how we should pray. There is no one set formula.

Evaluate your motives for praying. Asking wrongly means that we have selfish motives; we put ourselves first rather than genuine love for others. James 4:3 says, "You ask and do not receive, because you ask wrongly, to spend it on your passions."

Ask for forgiveness. If we harbor things in our hearts that should not be there—resentment, anger, hatred, envy, deceit, and the like—we must acknowledge and confess these things to God. A lifestyle of sin interferes with our prayers, as is clearly noted in the following passages:

> We know that God does not listen to sinners, but if anyone is a worshiper of God and does his will, God listens to him. (John 9:31)

> But your iniquities have made a separation between you and your God, and your sins have hidden his face from you so that he does not hear. (Isaiah 59:2)

> The LORD is far from the wicked, but he hears the prayer of the righteous. (Proverbs 15:29)

> If I had cherished iniquity in my heart, the Lord would not have listened. (Psalm 66:18)

The good news is that Jesus acknowledges those who repent and offers forgiveness. As mentioned earlier, I John 1:9 says, "If we confess our sins, he is faithful and just to forgive us our sins and to cleanse us from all unrighteousness." We must forgive others. If someone wrongs us, it is of utmost importance that we forgive that person. In the Lord's prayer, Jesus said, "Forgive us our sins as we forgive the sins of others." If we fail to forgive, neither will God forgive us. By not forgiving others, we render our prayers ineffective. In Mark 11:25, Jesus said, "And whenever you stand praying, forgive, if you have anything against anyone, so that your Father also who is in heaven may forgive you your trespasses."

Pray in faith. God proved over and over that there is no limit to His power and greatness. The many miracles described in the Bible attest to this. Jeremiah 32:17 acknowledges this: "Ah, Sovereign LORD, you have made the heavens and the earth by your great power and outstretched arm. Nothing is too hard for you." And Luke 1:37 similarly states, "For nothing will be impossible with God." God desires that we simply believe that He is able to do difficult things for us. We must trust Him completely and put our faith in Him. In Matthew 21:22, we read, "And whatever you ask in prayer, you will receive, if you have faith." Also, in James 1:6–7, it says, "But let him ask in faith, with no doubting, for the one who doubts is like a wave of the sea that is driven and tossed by the wind. For that person must not suppose that he will receive anything from the Lord." Similarly, we are to pray with confidence. Hebrews 4:16 says, "Let us then with confidence draw near to the throne of grace, that we may receive mercy and find grace to help in time of need." Acts 12:5 says, "So Peter was kept in prison, but earnest prayer for him was made to God by the church." James 5:18 says, "Elijah was a man with a nature like ours, and he prayed fervently that it might not rain, and for three years and six months it did not rain on the earth. Then he prayed again, and heaven gave rain, and the earth bore its fruit." Ask in Jesus's name. John 14:13 says, "Whatever you ask in my name, this I will do, that the Father may be glorified in the Son." Jesus has authority over all things in this world. When we pray in His name, we are acknowledging that there is nothing beyond His power and control.

Be persistent. Luke 18:1 says, "And he told them a parable to the effect that they ought always to pray and not lose heart." First Thessalonians 5:17 says, "Pray without ceasing," and in Colossians 4:2, we read "Continue steadfastly in prayer, being watchful in it with thanksgiving." Finally, in 1 Thessalonians 5:16–18, it says, "Rejoice always, pray without ceasing, give thanks in all circumstances; for this is the will of God in Christ Jesus for you." It may require hours, days, weeks, months, years, or even decades of prayer. Our role is to be faithful in prayer, regardless of how long it takes.

Pray alone and with others. Matthew 6:6 says, "But when you pray, go into your room and shut the door and pray to your Father who is in secret. And your Father who sees in secret will reward you." And Mark 1:35 says, "And rising very early in the morning, while it was still dark, he departed and went out to a desolate place, and there he prayed." But we also should pray with others. In Matthew 18:19–20, we read, "Again I say to you, if two of you agree on earth about anything they ask, it will be done for them by my Father in heaven. For where two or three are gathered in my name, there am I among them."

Don't hold back. God invites us to pray and wants us to bring everything to him. He truly means everything. I have learned over the years that God is interested even in the small things. As we read the Bible, we begin to realize that God is sovereign over and interested in even seemingly insignificant details. We may think that things are too small for God to care. Those who do so are missing out on seeing how God works in the significant and seemingly little things in our lives. Below is a thought starter list of things you can bring to God in prayer.

health	family	friends
faith	decisions	enemies
wisdom	God's presence	deliverance
salvation	employment	business
guidance	political leaders	healing
protection	peace	neighbors
anxiety	forgiveness	food
finances	employment	marriage
relationships	children	basic needs
career	conflict	gratitude

These items illustrate how prayer helps us in practical ways for everyday life. God listens to each request and provides answers in countless ways—all because He loves us.

FINDING WISDOM

The Bible teaches us how to gain wisdom. Wisdom is that virtue that is attained through knowledge and experience and then applied to various situations so that wise advice, choices, or decisions can be made. Biblical wisdom, while similar, has two key differences. The Bible indicates that that there is a source of wisdom, namely God. And it is something that can be given to us by God. We gain earthly wisdom through knowledge and experience, but there is a wisdom that runs far deeper than that. God's wisdom is superior to human wisdom in every way, and if we are to become truly wise, we must do it with God's help. Proverbs chapter 2 describes how this is accomplished. Biblical wisdom means learning to see things as God sees them and making choices or giving counsel as God would have us do. It means applying our knowledge in wise and meaningful ways. There are a number of actions we must take, such as fear God (show reverence and respect), listen to God, request it, search for it as for treasure, accept God's words as wise, and apply God's Word in our hearts. If we do, God will impart wisdom. Wisdom, then, is something to be pursued and received from God. In Jeremiah 33:3, we read "Call to me and I will answer you, and will tell you great and hidden things that you have not known." God reveals thing to us that we would otherwise not understand.

Wisdom is truly worth pursuing. One of the greatest compliments a person can receive is being asked for advice because of their wisdom. It is one of life's most valued virtues. In Proverbs 3:13–18, Solomon states that nothing you desire can compare with wisdom; it is more valuable than silver, gold, or rubies. Why is wisdom so valuable? In Proverbs 2:7–16, several benefits of wisdom are described. These are victory for the upright, God's protection, deliverance from evil, riches, honor, and blessings to all those who attain it. It means seeking God's advice for every situation rather than relying on our own knowledge. God's advice always yields a better outcome than our own. Proverbs 3:13–14 states, "Blessed are those who find wisdom, those who gain understanding, for she is more profitable than silver and yields better returns than gold."

Why is wisdom so valuable and how do we utilize this wisdom? Here are a few of the areas:

1. Wisdom about work. We are to work with diligence, with honesty, and to the best of our ability. Hard work brings rewards, and God gives our work meaning and success. For example, in Proverbs 14:23, it says, "All hard work brings a profit, but mere talk leads only to poverty" (NIV). And in Proverbs 12:11, we read, "Those

who work their land will have abundant food, but those who chase fantasies have no sense" (NIV).

2. Wisdom about wealth. The accumulation of wealth is not evil in itself, but we must recognize that it comes from God, and we are to honor Him with it. It is not the most important thing in life. Proverbs 27:24 says, "for riches do not endure forever and does a crown endure for all generations." It is not wealth that should be our focus; it is eternity. Wise individuals plan carefully, give generously, and honor God with their wealth.

3. Wisdom about words. Words have great potential for both good and evil. God cares about what we say, so we need to choose our words wisely by building up and not tearing down. Proverbs 25:11 says, "A word fitly spoken is like apples of gold in settings of silver." Words truly make a difference, and God will help us speak wisely, if we ask Him.

4. Wisdom about marriage. Marriage can bring either great satisfaction or great misery. Unfaithfulness destroys both the marriage and the unfaithful. Proverbs 18:22 says, "He who finds a wife finds what is good and receives favor from the Lord" (NIV). Of course, the same can be said for a husband. A faithful marriage partner is a gift from God and brings blessings. God grants us wisdom in finding that partner, if we ask Him.

5. Wisdom about relationships. The book of Proverbs has numerous verses about this. For example, it teaches us to choose our friends wisely (Proverbs 12:26) and being a faithful friend (Proverbs 17:17). Perhaps the most important advice on relationships is simply to keep one's focus on Jesus and obey all that He taught us, especially loving one another (John 13:34–35).

6. Wisdom about character. This is wonderfully described in Proverbs chapter 8, where it describes a wise person as having character traits such as righteousness, integrity, humility, and self-discipline. For example, in verse 7, we read, "My mouth speaks what is true, for my lips detest wickedness." These and other traits are attainable with God's help.

7. Wisdom about life. Ecclesiastes 7:12 states, "For the protection of wisdom is like the protection of money, and the advantage of knowledge is that wisdom preservers the life of him who has it." Unlike money, wisdom enhances our spiritual life and prepares us to serve God in spite of obstacles. And in Proverbs 20:5, we read, "The purpose in a man's heart is like deep water, but a man of understanding will draw it out."

For those who seek and find wisdom, benefits and blessings abound, and it enables them to navigate through life with God leading. Wisdom is a wonderful traveling companion.

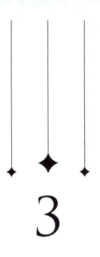

3

DEVELOPING PERSONAL CHARACTER

For this very reason, make every effort to add to your faith goodness;
and to goodness, knowledge; and to knowledge, self-control; and
to self-control, perseverance; and to perseverance, godliness; and
to godliness, mutual affection; and to mutual affection, love.
—1 Peter 1:5–7

God is deeply interested in our personal development. He wants us to become the best that we can be—in His eyes. Therefore, He provided teaching, guidance, and many examples of personal character so that we can both understand and *see* what these character traits are like. He wants us to grow and develop because as we do, we bring honor and glory to Him and become a blessing to others. As you will see in this chapter, we have the perfect example to follow, Jesus Christ. Jesus came to earth to bring salvation to all of humankind. But a secondary purpose was to demonstrate what "right living" means. He flawlessly modeled the kind of life to which we should aspire. The other feature of this chapter (and all others) is that we are never alone. We have a helper in the person of the Holy Spirit. Before He left this earth, Jesus promised that each of His followers would be given the Holy Spirit, who comes to dwell within us. One of His tasks is to guide us toward Christlikeness. He knows about all our weaknesses and the distractions of the world and helps us to learn and grow. This is a learning process that continues throughout our lives.

COURAGE

Many words help capture the meaning of courage, such as bravery in the face of hardship or danger, standing up for what is right, being resolute, and staying with one's conviction no matter the consequences. Often, courage is referred to when someone acts with valor in the line of duty (e.g., police or military) when facing danger. But courage can occur in almost any situation or circumstance. For example, it can take courage to forgive, apologize, take action, explore, confront someone, or face illness. In the Bible, we see many of these situations where courage is on display. As we examine these, we find that the Bible considers not only the act of courage but also the motivation—what enables courage. In every case, it includes God. We see both the motivation for courage (serving God) and God Himself involved in acts of bravery. Let us briefly examine a few of the many ways that courage is on display in the Bible.

Courage in Combat

When preparing Joshua to take over the leadership of the Israelites, Moses said these words to him in Deuteronomy 31:6, "Be strong and courageous. Do not fear or be in dread of them, for it is the LORD your God who goes with you. He will not leave you or forsake you." While there may have been reason for Joshua and the people to be afraid, they are instructed again and again to take courage and not be afraid, even though they would soon be engaging armies stronger than themselves. They were to take courage because God was with them. He would help them fight their battles. When the time came to actually cross the Jordan River and enter the land that God had promised them, God said these words to Joshua: "Have I not commanded you? Be strong and courageous. Do not be frightened, and do not be dismayed, for the LORD your God is with you wherever you go" (Joshua 1:9). Throughout Joshua's tenure as leader, courage was indeed on display—with God's help. Later, in Joshua 10:25, it was Joshua's turn to encourage the people, and he provides the key reason why they should be full of courage. "And Joshua said to them, 'Do not be afraid or dismayed; be strong and courageous. For the LORD will do this to all your enemies against whom you fight.'" God was personally involved in the battles. He promised, and it was so. This same God is available for our battles too, if we ask Him. Lastly, in 2 Chronicles 32:7, it says, "Be strong and courageous. Do not be afraid or dismayed before the king of Assyria and all the hordes that are with him, for there are more with us than with him." Having God on your side changes everything.

Courage When Making Decisions

Sometimes we face decisions that seem especially difficult to us. That is often because there is some measure of uncertainty and even risk involved; we are not sure of the best course of action. Courage is often necessary to make the right choice. This was true for Queen Esther. Though a foreigner (Hebrew), she became queen of the Persian Empire. During her reign, a plot was exposed that involved the king's top adviser planning to destroy the Hebrew people who were living as captives in Babylon. Should she or shouldn't she get involved to save here people from great harm? She chose the former, even though it could have meant losing her life. If the king was displeased with her, it could result in punishment by death. Her uncle Mordecai had urged Queen Esther to approach the king on behalf of her people. In Esther 4:15–16, she spoke these words to Mordecai: "Then Esther told them to reply to Mordecai, 'Go, gather all the Jews to be found in Susa, and hold a fast on my behalf, and do not eat or drink for three days, night or day. I and my young women will also fast as you do. Then I will go to the king, though it is against the law, and if I perish, I perish.'" The king's response was favorable to Queen Esther, and the end result was the protection of her people from a mass killing. As we study this historical event, it becomes abundantly clear that God was involved with every detail that occurred. Esther showed great courage in her decision. This amazing story can be found in the book of Esther.

A second example of decision courage was demonstrated by Daniel and three close friends during their exile in Babylon. Daniel and his friends were selected to eat at the king's table as part of their training (Daniel 1). They made the decision to refuse the food and drink (considered unclean), even though they could be severely punished for this act of defiance. But

God's hand was with them. He not only protected them but enabled them to excel in their training and become distinguished servants in the royal palace. Throughout the Bible, we see God's abundant blessings on those who are courageous for Him.

Courage When Sharing the Good News about Jesus

It often requires courage to talk about Jesus with those who do not know Him. In some places, the cost may be emotional or physical pain or both. Some even lose their lives. Jesus's disciples understood this but nevertheless spoke boldly and persistently wherever they went. They counted the cost, but their courage overcame all fear. They were ordinary men, but they accomplished extraordinary things. The apostle Paul, who experienced lashes, stoning, beatings, shipwrecks, and rejection, said these words: "Only let your manner of life be worthy of the gospel of Christ, so that whether I come and see you or am absent, I may hear of you that you are standing firm in one spirit, with one mind striving side by side for the faith of the gospel" (Philippians 1:27). This "manner of life," as Paul describes it, seldom comes naturally for most and requires courage. Paul realized that there was something much better that awaited him—eternal life in heaven. He heeded the words of Jesus in Matthew 10:28, "And do not fear those who kill the body but cannot kill the soul. Rather fear him who can destroy both soul and body in hell." As Paul wrote in Romans 8:31–39, "If God is for us, who can be against us … For I am convinced that neither death nor life, neither angels nor demons, neither the present nor the future, nor any powers, neither height nor depth, nor anything else in all creation, will be able to separate us from the love of God that is in Christ Jesus our Lord."

Courage When Facing Temptation

Temptations surround us each day. We are often tempted by things that are unwise, unhealthy, illegal, or even dangerous. Sometimes these temptations are so strong that it is difficult to resist them. But resisting is always possible. In 1 Corinthians 10:13, Paul wrote, "No temptation has overtaken you that is not common to man. God is faithful, and he will not let you be tempted beyond your ability, but with the temptation he will also provide the way of escape, that you may be able to endure it." An excellent example of this comes from the Old Testament, Joseph. He was sold into slavery and became a servant of one of the Pharaoh's officials, Potiphar. One day, Potiphar's wife attempted to seduce Joseph. But Joseph fled from her; he had the courage to resist. Although Joseph did the right thing, he was falsely accused of making sexual advances by Potiphar's wife and put in prison. Having the courage to resist temptation may create challenges for us. We may lose friends, be ridiculed, and more. In the end, Joseph's faithfulness resulted in his release from prison and elevation to second in command in all of Egypt. People may not notice the effort that is required to resist temptation, but God does.

Courage to Speak the Truth in Love

In Ephesians 4:15, Paul wrote, "Instead, speaking the truth in love, we will grow to become in every respect the mature body of him who is the head, that is, Christ." There is a tendency to either not speak the truth or speak the truth but not in love. Neither is acceptable. For those who know Christ, they know the truth and must speak it consistently but also must do so in love—with gentleness and respect. Jesus never told people only what they wanted to hear but rather what they needed to hear. On many occasions, Jesus used strong words that were shocking and even deemed offensive. For example, Jesus called the religious leaders (Pharisees and Sadducees) hypocrites (Matthew 23:1–12) and a brood of vipers (Matthew 12:34). Another time, a rich young ruler asked Jesus what he needed to do to inherit eternal life. Jesus knew his heart and instructed him to sell his possessions and follow Him. This saddened the young man; this was not what he wanted to hear (Matthew 19:16–22). When Jesus met a woman at a community well, He spoke the truth in love by sharing the good news with her and exposing her life of multiple divorces marriages (John 4:1–40). In each case, Jesus seemed harsh at times, but He loved all whom he encountered. Truth may be difficult to hear, but when done in love, it can have a sweet fragrance. Proverbs 27:6 puts it this way: "wounds from a friend can be trusted, but an enemy multiplies kisses."

Courage to Stand Firm in One's Faith

Perhaps one of the most inspiring verses in the Bible was spoken by Joshua near the end of his life. The Israelites had entered and conquered the land they were promised by God. In Joshua 24:15, we read, "But if serving the LORD seems undesirable to you, then choose for yourselves this day whom you will serve, whether the gods your ancestors served beyond the Euphrates, or the gods of the Amorites, in whose land you are living. But as for me and my household, we will serve the LORD." Joshua knew that the people would be tempted to abandon their God in favor of false gods and challenged the people to stand firm in their faith. Joshua stood firm in his faith in God and made it clear that his choice had been made. Challenges to one's faith come from all angles and forms. Standing firm may be very unpopular and go against societal norms. But for those who understand scripture and believe in God with all their hearts, they are not swayed by public opinion or criticism. They have the courage to stand fast in their faith because they are grounded in truth.

Courage When Threatened with Physical or Emotional Harm

There is a remarkable story in Daniel chapter 3 about three young men who were captives in Babylon. One day, they were told they must bow down to a statue of King Nebuchadnezzar or face execution. The three men refused to bow down. In verses 16–18, we find their response. "Shadrach, Meshach, and Abednego answered and said to the king, 'O Nebuchadnezzar, we have no need to answer you in this matter. If this be so, our God whom we serve is able to deliver us from the burning fiery furnace, and he will deliver us out of your hand, O king. But even if He does not, be it known to you, O king, that we will not serve your gods or worship the golden image that you have set up.'" They found the courage to defy a mighty king who had the power to take their lives. Or rather, they found the courage to remain faithful to God in the face of great personal danger. Such courage is grounded in a strong faith in God, who is vastly more powerful and mighty than any king (or anyone else) on earth.

Courage When Afraid of the Future

At times, the future can instill fear in us. We become fearful of what might happen (or not happen) and wonder how things will turn out. The Bible teaches that we can take heart because of a critically important truth: the future is in God's hands, and He knows and does what is best for us. In Matthew 5:34, Jesus said, "Therefore do not worry about tomorrow, for tomorrow will worry about itself. Each day has enough trouble of its own." We can face all the tomorrows with confidence and trust because of the fact that God is sovereign and reigns over all the earth. In James 4:13–14, we are reassured about the future: "Come now, you who say, 'Today or tomorrow we will go into such and such a town and spend a year there and trade and make a profit'—yet you do not know what tomorrow will bring. What is your life? For you are a mist that appears for a little time and then vanishes. Instead you ought to say, 'If the Lord wills, we will live and do this or that.'" We are to trust that God is involved with and controls the future. And lastly, in Jeremiah 29:11, we read, "For I know the plans I have for you, declares the LORD, plans for welfare and not for evil, to give you a future and a hope." We can be confident in the future because God, who is omniscient, sees the future perfectly. During the transition in leadership from David to his son Solomon, David said these reassuring words to Solomon, who wondered if he was up to the task of leading the nation: "Then David said to Solomon his son, 'Be strong and courageous and do it. Do not be afraid and do not be dismayed, for the LORD God, even my God, is with you. He will not leave you or forsake you, until all the work for the service of the house of the LORD is finished'" (1 Chronicles 28:20). We can face the future with courage and confidence because we know who holds the future in His hands. Philippians 4:13 says, "I can do all things through him who strengthens me."

Courage to Pray

There may be times when it becomes difficult to pray. This may be because we are afraid that God will say no, God will say yes, we do not feel worthy, or because we are simply afraid to come into the presence of our Almighty God because of something we did. No matter the reason, there are times when we must pray with courage. David expressed this in 1 Chronicles 17:25: "You my God have revealed to your servant that you will build a house for him. So your servant has found the courage to pray to you" (NIV). David was greatly humbled that God would think so highly of him, in spite of his failures, and that He would give the honor of building the temple to his son Solomon. God is merciful, loving, kind, and gracious in spite of our weaknesses and invites us to bring everything to Him in prayer. Everything! We are told to come boldly, come often, come humbly with whatever is on our heart. And He will listen. Remember these words from Psalm 27:14: "Wait for the LORD; be strong, and let your heart take courage; wait for the LORD!"

These are a few of the ways in which courage is on display in the Bible. As mentioned earlier, courage comes into play in many of life's circumstances. We can be strong and courageous throughout our lives if we put our hope and trust in Jesus. We must remember these words from Joshua 1:9: "Have I not commanded you? Be strong and courageous. Do not be afraid; do not be discouraged, for the LORD your God will be with you wherever you go." With God's help, we can courageously face anything in this life. We can overcome because Jesus already has.

FAITHFULNESS

Faithfulness involves the act of being faithful to someone or something. It means being true to your word, loyal, trustworthy, or authentic. It is something that all would agree is an admirable human characteristic. We desire faithfulness in marriage, friendships, employees, and even with pets. In as much as it is desirable, however, it can be elusive. It seems that faithfulness can give way to unfaithfulness all too easily or that faithfulness is inconsistent.

We can begin to understand what faithfulness is and why it is so important by looking at the standard of faithfulness as revealed in the Bible—God Himself. Faithfulness is part of God's character; it is His very nature to be faithful. This will never change, and we see this demonstrated throughout history, beginning in the first book, Genesis, to the last book, Revelation. We see God giving His word and then keeping His word soon thereafter, years later, centuries later, or even millennia later. Scripture shows that He has never failed to keep His promises. For example, God was faithful to Noah by protecting his family from the flood. He was faithful to the promises (covenants) He made to Abraham by providing numerous offspring and being a blessing to all nations, which came to pass through Jesus Christ. God was faithful to the all prophets whom He directed to bring warnings and promises of hope to His people by always remaining true to His word. What He said came to pass. He was faithful to the kings in the Old Testament by answering their prayers and protecting them, even though many were unfaithful to Him. He promised to provide help, guidance, forgiveness, blessings, and love, and He has done all of these and so much more. God remained faithful to hundreds of prophecies written in the Old Testament about the birth, death, and resurrection of Jesus Christ. Every one of them came to pass. God demonstrated His faithfulness by providing a Savior for all people for all time. Jesus exhibited this same standard of faithfulness during His life on earth. He was faithful to His disciples, to the Father, and to His promises of suffering and death. Faithfulness is part of God's nature; it is who He is.

The author of Psalm 100 wrote these words in verse 5: "For the Lord is good and his love endures forever; his faithfulness continues through all generations" (NIV). He is faithful with His promises, love, kindness, forgiveness, justice, and mercy. In Lamentations 3:22–23, the prophet Jeremiah wrote these words: "Because of the Lord's great love we are not consumed, for his compassions never fail. They are new every morning; great is your faithfulness" (NIV). He wrote these words after the city of Jerusalem had been destroyed. Many in it were killed, and many others were exiled to Babylon. Jeremiah emphasized God's faithfulness because

God promised that He would restore the city in the future, and Jeremiah believed Him. Indeed, it came to pass many years later. God was faithful, and this continued throughout generation after generation. But even beyond that, He has demonstrated His faithfulness to every generation since the beginning of recorded history. And His faithfulness continues today in your and my life and will continue with our descendants. God is the standard for faithfulness. God's faithfulness is truly great and for all generations. How then should we respond to God's faithfulness? Following are three ways that we can put faithfulness into practice.

Given that faithfulness is inherent to God's nature, we, being created in His image, are expected to exhibit faithfulness toward God. This is made clear in the following passages: Joshua 24:14 says, "Now fear the Lord and serve him with all faithfulness." Joshua 24:14 says, "Now therefore fear the Lord and serve him in sincerity and in faithfulness. Put away the gods that your fathers served beyond the River and in Egypt, and serve the Lord." And in Proverbs 3:3, we are told these words: "Let love and faithfulness never leave you." Though imperfectly, we show our faithfulness to God by being obedient to Him, praying to Him, and worshipping Him. In the Old Testament, God gave us the Ten Commandments; our task is to faithfully obey these throughout our lives. In the New Testament, Jesus also gave a number of commands, such as loving one another, and we are expected to obey these as well. But God also asks certain things of us during our lifetime. For example, God calls us to certain ministries, such as teaching, preaching, evangelizing, helping the poor, and many others. We demonstrate our faithfulness to God by being obedient to His callings. Some are called to leave everything behind and serve in foreign countries under extremely difficult circumstances. We respond to God's faithfulness by being obedient and faithful to Him. God gives us special gifts and abilities to benefit others, and we are expected to use these faithfully. God provides material resources (e.g., wealth), and we are expected to give cheerfully to the church and to those in need. In the Bible, there is an abundance of examples of individuals who demonstrated their faithfulness to God.

- Abraham trusted God and left his home and relatives to move to the land of Canaan.
- Noah was faithful by spending many decades of his life building an ark.
- Moses was faithful by leading his people to the land God promised them.
- Samuel was faithful by entering full-time service in the temple.
- Prophets like Elijah and Elisha faithfully proclaimed God's messages in the face of personal threats.
- Daniel was faithful to God by not defiling himself with food offered to idols.

The above characters were faithful to God, as demonstrated by their obedience. We too can demonstrate our faithfulness to God through our obedience. In John 14:15, Jesus said, "If you love me, you will keep my commandments." Just as Jesus's life exhibited faithfulness throughout, our lives must be characterized by faithfulness. We do this by putting Jesus's commands into action, such as forgiving others, loving others, showing mercy, and being compassionate. We are also expected to be faithful in our places of worship, as demonstrated by stewardship of money, serving others, and participation in worship.

When we are faithful to God, He blesses us abundantly. Note the following verses:

Let not steadfast love and faithfulness forsake you; bind them around your neck; write them on the tablet of your heart. So you will find favor and good success in the sight of God and man. (Proverbs 3:3–4)

A faithful man will abound with blessings. (Proverbs 28:20)

The Lord rewards every man for his righteousness and faithfulness. (1 Samuel 26:23)

And the Lord said, Who then is the faithful and wise manager, whom his master will set over his household, to give them their portion of food at the proper time? Blessed is that servant whom his master will find so doing when he comes. Truly, I say to you, he will set him over all his possessions. (Luke 12:42–44)

The Bible also teaches that we are to be faithful to one another. We are to be faithful to our spouses, our extended families, neighbors, employers, and the like. Consider the last five commands found in Exodus 20 (summarized): Never take the life of a fellow human being. Do not hate people or hurt them with words and actions. Do not have sexual relations with anyone other than your spouse. God forbids sex outside of marriage. Don't even look lustfully at others. Rather, treat your body and the bodies of others with respect. Never steal or take anything that doesn't belong to you without permission. Never tell a lie about someone or accuse someone falsely. Always tell the truth. Never be jealous of anything that belongs to others. Be content and thankful with what God has given you. These, along with Jesus's commands to love and forgive one another, demonstrate our faithfulness to God and to others. Those who follow these can be trusted by family, friends, and neighbors. People can believe our words and be confident that we will not do things that will cause harm.

Faithfulness, then, is of utmost importance. Consider this. If God did not exhibit His faithfulness, we would not be able to trust what is taught in the Bible. We would never know for sure if His promises will come true, and our hope in the future would be uncertain. But we know that, as previously mentioned, God's faithfulness continues through all generations. God does not change, as stated about Jesus in Hebrews 13:8: "Jesus Christ is the same yesterday and today and forever." By striving to be faithful in our lives, by being true to our word, loyal, and authentic, we exhibit the character of Jesus in our lives, which enables others to be able to trust us.

GENEROSITY

There has been and always will be a strong desire to hold on tightly to money. The reasons for this are many and sometimes complex. Perhaps it is because we think it gives us power and status. It may be that we love the things it can buy or because we love money more than anything else. It could be because some of us tend to hoard things or feelings of insecurity. One might say, what if I lose my job? What if there is a financial crisis? What if my health fails? What if …? We are never quite sure about tomorrow and wonder if we will have enough. Whatever the reason, letting go of our resources does not come easily for many. Even those who are wealthy worry about money.

The Bible has much to say about overcoming the grip that money can have on us. In the Old Testament, giving was a command from God called a tithe. A tithe literally meant a tenth of something, which could be considered income but also a harvest of crops or livestock. For example, it was expected that the first tenth of yield was given to God. Thus, the harvester gave because it was a required and out of gratitude for God's provisions. It also meant that the giver trusted that God would provide the remaining 90 percent of the harvest. In addition to giving a tenth, people were encouraged to give gifts above and beyond that in the form of freewill offerings. These were given out of deep gratitude for what God had provided but also because it simply brought joy to their hearts. In Deuteronomy 16:17, it says, "Every man shall give as he is able, according to the blessing of the LORD your God that he has given you." Tithing was an act of obedience because it demonstrated trust in God. They learned that giving was not a burden but rather a pleasure; they gave generously.

Old Testament giving had multiple purposes. It provided the resources for priests and Levites to live and carry out their tasks, reminded people of their trust in God, and allowed for the demonstration of God's faithfulness to His people. It also served to teach people to avoid becoming too attached to their possessions. Giving away one's wealth helps prevent selfishness and self-centeredness. The underlying theme of Old Testament giving was not merely one of duty but, rather, something that came from the heart. Another reason is found in Proverbs 19:17, where it says, "Whoever is generous to the poor lends to the LORD, and he will repay him for his deed." Giving not only helped those in need but also yielded a blessing to the giver. And in Malachi 3:10, it says, "Bring the full tithe into the storehouse, that there may be food in my house. And thereby put me to the test, says the LORD of hosts, if I will not open the windows of heaven for you and pour down for you a blessing until there is no more need." And in Proverbs 3:9–10, it says, "Honor the LORD with your wealth and with the first fruits of all your produce; then your barns will be filled with plenty, and your vats will be bursting with wine." Here, it's not only a challenge by God to give generously but also the promise of blessings for those who help others.

In the New Testament, the topic of money and giving is mentioned numerous times by Jesus, and later by his disciples. Jesus understood the control that money can have over people, and He made it clear that we are to love God more than money. He instructed us to store treasures in heaven rather than earth. One important way we store up these treasures in heaven is by giving to those who are in need. In Luke 12:33–34, Jesus said, "Sell your possessions and give to the poor. Provide purses for yourselves that will not wear out, a treasure in heaven that will not be exhausted, where no thief comes near and no moth destroys. For where your treasure is, there your heart will be also" (NIV). In another passage, Jesus taught that by helping those in need, we serve not only them but also Jesus. "Then the righteous will answer him, 'Lord, when did we see you hungry and feed you, or thirsty and give you something to drink? When did we see you a stranger and invite you in, or needing clothes and clothe you? When did we see you sick or in prison and go to visit you?' The King will reply, 'I tell you the truth, whatever you did for one of the least of these brothers of mine, you did for me'" (Matthew 25:37–40). One day, Jesus encountered a rich man who asked Jesus what he needed to do to enter the kingdom of God. The rich man said that he kept all the laws faithfully. "When Jesus heard this, he said to him, 'You still lack one thing. Sell everything you have and give to the poor, and you will have treasure in heaven. Then come, follow me.' When he heard this, he became very sad, because he was a man of great wealth. Jesus looked at him and said, 'How hard it is for the rich to enter the kingdom of God!'" (Luke 18:22–24). Jesus recognized that the man loved money more than God. It was too difficult for him to part with his wealth to help others. When we give a portion of wealth to help others, it demonstrates that we have true control over our possessions rather than being controlled by them.

While being generous is important, it is also important to give cheerfully. In Corinthians 2:9, the apostle Paul wrote, "Each of you should give what you have decided in your heart to give, not reluctantly or under compulsion, for God loves a cheerful giver." Giving comes from the heart and should be done with gladness. Giving should not be done because we ought to, we feel pressured, or, worse, to impress others, for this undermines the act of giving. The principle is that we give out of love and gratitude to God for who He is and what He has done for us. And it is to be done with a genuine desire to help and serve others. Moreover, God is not as interested in our actual giving amounts as He is in our giving attitude. Generous giving became evident in the early church, as described in Acts 2:44–45: "And all who believed were together and had all things in common. And they were selling their possessions and belongings and distributing the proceeds to all, as any had need." There was great unity and oneness of spirit. No one lacked because genuine love as demonstrated in the form of generosity prevailed. Giving is an act of worship; we honor God with our wealth (Proverbs 3:9).

The Bible teaches that those who do not give or give sparingly have an issue with the heart. It comes down to whether we love money more than God. Jesus said you cannot serve two masters (Matthew 6:24); you cannot love both God and money equally. In the example mentioned earlier regarding the wealthy ruler, Jesus challenged him to give away his possessions and follow Him. The ruler went away sad. Why couldn't he be generous with his possessions? Jesus knew what the issue was—the ruler loved his money more than God. This is all too common in every culture, especially with those who have wealth. Giving of one's possessions may not be easy, but it is essential that we do. The wisdom found in Proverbs 28:22 is a wonderful reminder for all of us. "A stingy man hastens after wealth and does not know that poverty will come upon him." On the other hand, generous giving is honoring to God. In Proverbs 22:9, it says, "Whoever has a bountiful eye will be blessed, for he shares his bread with the poor." God notices what and how we give, and He responds accordingly.

How then should we implement the principle of generosity? First, by examining our hearts and determining the amount. This is always a matter between you and God, and He will respond to your questions with guidance. Second, giving should be a joy, not a burden. If you give reluctantly or out of compulsion, it means that your heart is not in the right place. Evaluate your motives for giving and seek God's wisdom. He will be overjoyed to help you give from the heart. If you are giving for any reason other than a love for God and your neighbors, it is time for a change in attitude. Thirdly, give first to the local church and in the amount that provides peace and joy in your heart. Many people suggest the tithe as a guideline, as was taught in the Old Testament, but this should not be followed in a legalistic manner. God may direct you to a different amount, as was mentioned by the apostle Paul in 2 Corinthians 9:7, "Each one must give as he has decided in his heart, not reluctantly or under compulsion, for God loves a cheerful giver." Fourthly, give to individuals and/or organizations outside your local church. When you ask, God will direct where and how much.

As mentioned earlier, giving is a matter of the heart. Jesus clearly taught that the practice of giving pleases God, benefits others, and benefits us. In Luke 6:38, Jesus said, "Give, and it will be given to you. Good measure, pressed down, shaken together, running over, will be put into your lap. For with the measure you use it will be measured back to you." And in Acts 20:35, we find these words: "In all things I have shown you that by working hard in this way we must help the weak and remember the words of the Lord Jesus, how he himself said, 'It is more blessed to give than to receive.'" Not only should we give, but give generously from our hearts. When we do, the what-ifs melt away, and fears become peace and happiness.

HONESTY

An honest person strives toward being truthful. God loves honesty and intensely hates anything that is dishonest. This is not at all surprising because God is the standard of perfection. He is the perfect judge, who is able to discern between right and wrong. God wants and expects us to speak the truth, to always do the honorable thing, to never tell a lie, never cheat, never deceive, never bribe anyone or accept a bribe, and never speak untruthfully about someone. He commanded this in Leviticus 19:11, "You shall not steal; you shall not deal falsely; you shall not lie to one another." These and other commands comprise God's moral law, which was given in ancient times but applies equally well today.

The Bible teaches about being honest with words and actions. Our words matter to God. Consider the following proverbs about words:

> Whoever speaks the truth gives honest evidence, but a false witness utters deceit. (Proverbs 12:17)

> Lying lips are an abomination to the LORD, but those who act faithfully are his delight. (Proverbs 12:22)

> A false witness will not go unpunished, and he who breathes out lies will not escape. (Proverbs 19:5)

> Better is a poor person who walks in his integrity than one who is crooked in speech and is a fool. (Proverbs 19:1)

Note in Psalm 22:12 that when we speak honestly, it is pleasing to God. We may not know whether or not someone is speaking the truth, but God always does, even if something is only partly true. Moreover, He not only judges what can be heard but the intent behind the words—what is in the heart.

God always desires that all of our actions are honest as well. Consider the following wisdom from the book of Proverbs:

> A false balance is an abomination to the LORD, but a just weight is his delight. (Proverbs 11:1)

> The integrity of the upright guides them, but the crookedness of the treacherous destroys them. (Proverbs 11:3)

Better is a little with righteousness than great revenues with injustice. (Proverbs 16:18)

As with words, actions come from the heart. And our actions should align with our words. Honest words without honest actions are hollow and unacceptable to God.

Honesty is such an admirable quality that one would expect it to be the norm everywhere. This should not be so hard, should it—to always say and do the right thing? But sadly, it appears to be very difficult, judging by prevalence of dishonesty in our world. Perhaps one reason is because on the surface, dishonesty appears to actually have some benefit. Dishonesty may result in some advantage, such as financial or political gain. The Bible, however, warns that such gains are temporary, and in the end, the dishonest person ultimately loses. Proverbs 10:9 says, "Whoever walks in integrity walks securely, but he who makes his ways crooked will be found out." Though dishonesty may be hidden from other people, it is always known to God—always.

Why is honesty so important? There are many excellent reasons. First, honesty is expected of us. In 1 Peter 2:12, we read, "Keep your conduct among the Gentiles honorable, so that when they speak against you as evildoers, they may see your good deeds and glorify God on the day of visitation." In the Beatitudes, Jesus provided this special blessing in Matthew 5:8: "Blessed are the pure in heart, for they shall see God." A person who is pure in heart abides by God's rules.

Second, honesty leaves one with a clear conscience. In Hebrews 13:18, it says, "Pray for us, for we are sure that we have a clear conscience, desiring to act honorably in all things." And in Acts 24:16, we read, "So I always take pains to have a clear conscience toward both God and man." Dishonesty often leads to guilt and shame, robbing one of joy. But a clear conscience allows one to live at peace with one's self and with God.

Third, honesty promotes peace and unity between friends, within families, and within groups and churches. Consider Proverbs 16:28: "A dishonest man spreads strife, and a whisperer separates close friends. Dishonesty, on the other hand, results in mistrust and broken relationships." Also, in Philippians 4:8–9, we read, "Finally, brothers, whatever is true, whatever is honorable, whatever is just, whatever is pure, whatever is lovely, whatever is commendable, if there is any excellence, if there is anything worthy of praise, think about these things. What you have learned and received and heard and seen in me—practice these things, and the God of peace will be with you."

Fourth, honesty can bring recognition and reward from others, including superiors. Proverbs 16:13 says, "Righteous lips are the delight of a king, and he loves him who speaks what is right." To be recognized as an honest person is one of the greatest compliments anyone can receive; it does not go unnoticed.

Fifth, organizations of any kind, whether secular or religious, cannot last without honest leaders. They cannot properly function and risk collapse. When Moses was looking for leaders to appoint as judges, God provided these criteria in Exodus 18:21: "Moreover, look for able men from all the people, men who fear God, who are trustworthy and hate a bribe, and place such men over the people as chiefs of thousands, of hundreds, of fifties, and of tens." An honest leader is trustworthy, as is the organization they lead.

Sixth, honesty is something we inherently desire because that is what we seek in others. We want our family, friends, coworkers, leaders, and neighbors to be honest with us. In Matthew 7:12, Jesus said, "So whatever you wish that others would do to you, do also to them, for this is the Law and the Prophets." We call this the *golden rule* because it is of great value to people everywhere. In Galatians 6:7–8, the apostle Paul said, "Do not be deceived: God is not mocked, for whatever one sows, that will he also reap. For the one who sows to his own flesh will from the flesh reap corruption, but the one who sows to the Spirit will from the Spirit reap eternal life." If we sow seeds of dishonesty, chances are good that we will be treated in kind.

Lastly, a life of honesty imitates Jesus. There is no greater goal on earth than to be like Jesus. He is our example, our Lord, our master, our guide, and our friend. Jesus never said or did anything that was dishonest; honesty was (and is) inherent to His nature.

How can we live a life of honesty? Proverbs 3:5–6 (a Bible passage I refer to often) provides a wonderful and powerful guide for us. "Trust in the Lord with all your heart and do not lean on your own understanding. In all your ways acknowledge Him and He will direct your paths." If we trust God—with all our heart—He will guide us, with His own heart. He will help us to always do and say the right thing. If you ever have a question about choosing the right thing to do or say, simply ask God. He always listens and always guides. This passage also cautions us to avoid depending on our own understanding. We are limited in many ways and make mistakes. God's understanding, however, is perfect. Also, we must remember the golden rule found in Matthew 7:12, where we are commanded to do to others that which we would have them do to us. If we want others to always be honest with us, we must always do the same. That is always the best way and the way that Jesus would have us travel during life's journey.

What God desires are honest parents, spouses, mechanics, politicians, businesspeople, friends, teachers, leaders, employees, neighbors, and so on. In the Bible, He shows us how to accomplish this. It really isn't all that difficult once you make honesty a way of life.

KINDNESS

Words used to describe kindness include compassion, helpfulness or thoughtfulness, sympathy, mercy, being considerate, and more. Kindness means saying or doing nice things for others (animals too), with nothing expected in return. While the Bible does not specifically define kindness, the meaning becomes clear when we examine examples of kindness demonstrated by various Bible characters.

It is not surprising that we find many examples of kindness in the Bible because kindness originates from God; it is part of His nature. Throughout history, God has shown His kindness to us by His grace and mercy, deliverance, and compassion. It also is demonstrated by His great love for us. In many verses, God's kindness is linked with love, thus the term *loving-kindness*. For example, in Psalm 36:7, we read, "How precious is Your loving-kindness, O God! And the children of men take refuge in the shadow of Your wings" (NKJV). And in Psalm 69:16, it says, "Answer me, O Lord, for Your loving-kindness is good; according to the greatness of Your compassion, turn to me" (NKJV). It is not unusual to see the word *loving* precede *kindness* when referring to God. That is because God's kindness accompanies God's love for people. God loves all people deeply, and this is demonstrated by the kindness He has shown throughout history. His kindness was made manifest through protection, deliverance, forgiveness, and provisions during difficult times. God's kindness was further evidenced when Jesus came to earth. He was merciful to all people by providing a means of salvation and eternal life for everyone who believes.

Below are some ways that kindness is referred to in the Old and the New Testaments:

- A king was advised to show kindness to his subjects (2 Chronicles 10:7).
- The prophet Daniel advised King Nebuchadnezzar to be kind to the oppressed (Daniel 4:27).
- The apostle Paul taught that love is patient and love is kind (1 Corinthians13:4); challenged us to be kind, compassionate, and forgiving toward one another (Ephesians 4:32); and said that we are to be kind to everyone (2 Timothy 2:24).
- Anyone who withholds kindness from a friend forsakes the fear of the Almighty (Job 6:14).
- And in the book of Proverbs, we find many words of wisdom about kindness:

> a kind man benefits himself (11:17); an anxious heart weighs a man down, but a kind word cheers him up (12:25); blessed is he who is kind to the needy (14:21); whoever is kind to the needy honors God (14:31); he who is kind to the poor lends to the Lord and will reward him for what he has done (19:17);
> a kind woman gains respect (11:16).

In the New Testament, Jesus's life on earth provides the perfect example of kindness. Jesus loved others deeply, healed the sick and lame, and showed genuine concern for all people. For example, in Matthew 14:14, we read, "When He went ashore, He saw a large crowd, and felt compassion for them and healed their sick." He further demonstrated His loving-kindness to us by sacrificing himself on the cross so that we can have eternal life. That is the ultimate demonstration of loving-kindness—giving up your own life so that others may live. Therefore, in response to God's kindness to us, we are expected to show kindness to others.

There are many stories in the Old and New Testaments that illustrate kindness. King David provided two ways in which he showed kindness. The first takes place when Saul (the first king of Israel) became jealous of David because of David's military success. Saul was jealous of David and began hating him so much that he plotted to kill him. Saul's son Jonathan and David were close friends, and Jonathan showed kindness to David by warning him of his father's plot. Jonathan protected David's life while risking his own and enabled David to escape. This story is found in 1 Samuel 20:12–17. That was the last time David and Jonathan were together. Shortly thereafter, Jonathan was killed in battle along with his father.

A second example is found in 2 Samuel 9:1–13, where King David expressed a desire to show kindness to a member of Jonathan's family following Jonathan's death. David searched for a descendant of Jonathan and discovered he had a son, Mephibosheth, who was crippled in both feet. David showed him kindness by providing him with a place at his own table all his remaining days. He did this out of love and respect for his friend Jonathan and expected nothing in return.

A third example is found in the book of Ruth. Naomi's daughters-in-law showed kindness to her after her husband and two sons died and she was left destitute (Ruth 1:1–8). In verse 8, we read, "May the LORD show you kindness, as you have shown kindness to your dead husbands and to me." Naomi was a foreigner in their land, but her daughters-in-law treated her as they would their own mother.

Kindness is a fruit of the Spirit mentioned in Galatians 5:22–23. This means that our lives are expected to bear the fruit of kindness and are expected to do so often, to everyone and as long as we live. Showing kindness to others is what Jesus expects us to do. In fact, we are commanded to be kind. In Ephesians 4:32, it says, "Be kind and compassionate to one another, forgiving each other, just as in Christ God forgave you." We are to be kind to others by being compassionate and forgiving. The absence of kindness is an alternative that should be unacceptable to all.

How can we show kindness to others? We do this by our actions and by our words. It is by saying words that build up, encourage, show support, and demonstrate that we care. And it is by doing things for others, such as filling a need, forgiving, giving of your time, showing empathy, and doing something special for someone. There are opportunities to show kindness virtually every day, but it requires having a mindset of kindness so that it becomes natural. And whatever things we say or do must be done with genuine love, for this pleases God, the author of kindness.

MORALITY

Imagine a society in which actions such as lying, stealing, cheating, and assault were allowed or, worse, encouraged. And what if there was no basis for determining that these actions are wrong? That would be a most undesirable place in which to live. But there was such a place at one time. Early in history, the world was filled with so much evil and violence that God chose to destroy all people except for Noah and his immediate family. God was deeply opposed to all actions that He deemed evil, meaning they were in contrary to His moral law. He established clear standards for right and wrong in the Bible. And it was (and is) God's desire that we live our lives in accordance with His rules. He provided all that is necessary for us to make the right choices—to do and say what is right and avoid doing wrong. For example, God gave His Word (the Bible). And in the Bible are contained the Ten Commandments, which are key building blocks for moral behavior. These are summarized below:

1. Have no other gods but God.
2. Do not worship idols (things that replace God).
3. Do not blasphemy (take God's name in vain).

4. Keep the Sabbath holy.
5. Honor your father and mother.
6. Do not murder.
7. Do not commit adultery.
8. Do not steal.
9. Do not lie.
10. Do not covet.

These commandments establish the standard for right and wrong. Because God is perfect, He understands right and wrong perfectly and is the only authority capable of defining the rules. Moreover, God is the only possible source of these standards. Any other source would be arbitrary. How would we ever know something is morally wrong unless there is an absolute standard for declaring so?

In the New Testament, Jesus succinctly summarized the Ten Commandments in Luke 10:27, where He said, "'Love the Lord your God with all your heart and with all your soul and with all your strength and with all your mind'; and, 'Love your neighbor as yourself.'" Yes, that's it! It sounds simple, and it is. We are to maintain our complete focus on God and treat our neighbors as we would like to be treated. And in Matthew 7:12, Jesus put it this way: "So whatever you wish that others would do to you, do also to them, for this is the Law and the Prophets." The Bible teaches that we cannot keep all of God's commands perfectly; we all fall short. But when we acknowledge this, God extends His grace and forgives us.

Doing what is right according to our own standards is unacceptable to God. For instance, in Judges 17:6, it says, "In those days there was no king in Israel. Everyone did what was right in his own eyes." This drew the ire of God, and He brought judgment and punishment upon them. This actually occurred many times in that period because people continually forgot about God's moral law and did as they pleased. Also, In Isaiah 5:20, God warned us with these words: "Woe to those who call evil good and good evil, who put darkness for light and light for darkness, who put bitter for sweet and sweet for bitter!" The New Testament also has numerous warnings for those who fail to live by God's commands. We can know right from wrong, and we are held accountable for our actions. We must do what is right in God's eyes, not our own. In Galatians 5:19–21, Paul wrote, "Now the works of the flesh are evident: sexual immorality, impurity, sensuality, idolatry, sorcery, enmity, strife, jealousy, fits of anger, rivalries, dissensions, divisions, envy, drunkenness, orgies, and things like these. I warn you, as I warned you before, that those who do such things will not inherit the kingdom of God." Conversely, following God's commands were put into positive words by Paul in Philippians 4:8, where he wrote "Finally, brothers, whatever is true, whatever is honorable, whatever is just, whatever is pure, whatever is lovely, whatever is commendable, if there is any excellence, if there is anything worthy of praise, think about these things." There truly are moral absolutes for us, and these are described in scripture.

We have no excuse for not knowing right from wrong. God designed each of us with an ability to do this; we have something called a conscience. "Let your conscience be your guide" is a cliché that is sometimes used when faced with choices. Our conscience is something inside us that helps us decide the right thing to do. In Romans 2:15, Paul wrote, "They show that the work of the law is written on their hearts, while their conscience also bears witness, and their conflicting thoughts accuse or even excuse them." Of course we can ignore and override it at any time. Those who have belief in and follow Jesus also have a perfect helper at all times to guide their choices, that being the Holy Spirit. He teaches, guides, leads, helps, corrects (and much more) through life's choices. The Holy Spirit helps us make the right moral decision—if we listen to Him. He was sent to us by Jesus Himself to help us do God's will. (See John chapters 14 and 16.) There is never a reason or excuse for making poor moral choices in our lives, in any situation or circumstance. We are held accountable.

Not only are the standards for knowing right from wrong explicit in the Bible, but we also have excellent examples of individuals who lived moral (albeit imperfect) lives—Noah, Abraham, Job, the prophets Jeremiah, Daniel and Isaiah, and a host of others. Our ultimate example of course is Jesus. He is the only person who lived on earth who never sinned. He executed God's moral law perfectly. He provided a model for living a moral life for all people for all time. He taught us how to love, to forgive, to serve others, and to maintain complete focus on things above, not things on this earth. That is why those who are followers of Jesus try to be like Him. While they can never attain perfection here on earth, they do their best to live lives of obedience to Him. As stated earlier, we must

- love God with all our heart, soul, mind, and strength; and
- love our neighbor as ourselves.

If one truly loves God and truly loves all neighbors, that person would be obeying the intent of all ten commands. Thus, we would not lie, cheat, or steal because doing so dishonors God and would be evidence that we do not love our neighbors.

God's commands as revealed in the Bible provide the standards for moral living for people everywhere. One can know with certainty whether actions or words are right or wrong by studying the Bible, applying it to one's life, and listening to the Holy Spirit. The apostle John explained it this way in John 14:15: "If you love me, you will keep my commandments." The alternative is a lifestyle that compromises God's moral law. It is our choice to make. Proverbs 14:12 says, "There is a way that appears to be right, but in the end it leads to death" (NIV). God's way is always better.

PATIENCE

Someone who is patient remains calm under adverse circumstances. They face challenges calmly, without complaining and maintain self-control. Patience can also describe one's attitude toward situations—someone who is flexible, reasonable, nondemanding or not insisting that things go his or her own way. Many of us have a tendency to be impatient, to react hastily and strongly when confronted with things that get in our way. Simply put, we don't like to wait. Patience may not be an easy character trait to attain, but according to the Bible, it is very desirable.

We have much to learn about patience from the Bible because, like love, it is part of God's nature. He demonstrated patience with people and nations consistently and abundantly throughout biblical history. God was patient with Moses when Moses resisted God's command to lead the people out of Egypt. He was patient with the nation of Israel even though they disobeyed him repeatedly. God was patient with Job's long discussion with his friends, which was laden with unwarranted complaints about God. God was patient with Peter and the other disciples who were slow to understand many of Jesus's teachings and to believe in Him. And God has been especially patient with individuals like me who have made many mistakes. For all people who have ever lived or are alive today, God's patience means second chances and an opportunity to repent. Were it not for God's patience, we would all be in serious trouble. In 2 Peter 3:8–10, Peter explained the reasons for God's patience: "But do not forget this one thing, dear friends: With the Lord a day is like a thousand years, and a thousand years are like a day. The Lord is not slow in keeping his promise, as some understand slowness. He is patient with you, not wanting anyone to perish, but everyone to come to repentance." God is patient for our sake. His patience makes our salvation possible as well as our ongoing spiritual development. In Philippians 1:6, it says, "Being confident of this, that he who began a good work in you will carry it on to completion until the day of Christ Jesus."

Since God is patient with us, we too must be patient with others and in all situations. Patience should be an integral part of our character. Consider the following passages in Proverbs:

> A patient man has great understanding, but a quick-tempered man displays folly. (Proverbs 14:29)

> A hot-tempered person starts fights; a cool-tempered person stops them. (Proverbs 15:15 NLT)

> A person's wisdom yields patience; it is to one's glory to overlook an offense. (Proverbs 19:11 NIV)

> Through patience a ruler can be persuaded, and a soft tongue can break a bone. (Proverbs 25:15)

In these passages, we see that patience and wisdom go hand in hand.

It is the wise who exhibit patience in all areas of life. Patience enables us to bring calm to situations, make good choices, and influence others for the better. It helps us accomplish far more than if we acted in haste.

In scripture, patience often refers to long-suffering endurance. King David provides an example of what longsuffering means. He was pursued by Saul and his men for many months and endured great hardship. At times, he and his men were at the point of exhaustion while fleeing for their lives. Twice, David had the opportunity to end his plight by killing Saul. In the eyes of many, he would have been justified in doing so. But David chose to honor God's anointed and let him live. By doing so, he chose to extend his own suffering. He was patient and honored God's timing rather than his own. David's actions show how patience means active endurance anchored by hope and assurance. It is this quality that keeps people on firm footing during life's storms.

James 5:7–8 provides a wonderful illustration of patience: "See how the farmer waits for the land to yield its valuable crop and how patient he is for the autumn and spring rains. You too, be patient and stand firm, because the Lord's coming is near." Here, patience means endurance—staying focused until the goal is reached. Many other things require patience, such as patience for answers to prayer, patience for healing, or patience for something to change. Just as the farmer waits for the crop to ripen, trust that God will accomplish things in His timing. And God's timing is always perfect.

How then can we learn the virtue of patience? As with everything, the Bible provides guidance. First, we must seek God's wisdom through prayer. It may be a very short prayer in the moment or extended and repeated prayers. Ask God's advice on the matter. Remember that God's timing is perfect and trust that He will guide you. Also remember that you are not alone in any situation. The Holy Spirit is there to guide you each step of the way. He will teach, guide, and correct you—if you ask Him and listen to Him. Patience is a fruit of the Spirit, and He desires for you to excel in this. Second, learn from the example of others. Find someone who exhibits this quality and ask their advice. Third, find a mentor who can help and coach you to achieve a balance between impatience, action, and patience. Fourth, study all the scripture passages relating to patience and characters who struggled with and demonstrated patience.

Patience does not mean inaction. There is a place for impatience and action but also for patience. God does not want us to be passive and simply let things slide. He offers wisdom to act appropriately so that His will is done, not ours.

RESPECT FOR AUTHORITY

Showing respect means to value or honor someone. This is not a popular topic in some countries and cultures, and in some ways, it even goes contrary to our human nature. We love our independence. But the Bible teaches that respect for authority is essential at all levels and all types of authority, and there are good reasons why this is so. Let us examine what the Bible teaches about respect. There are at least six kinds of authority that deserve our respect that will be discussed here.

Respect for God

In numerous passages, we are instructed to respect and honor God. Exodus 20:7 states, "You shall not take the name of the LORD your God in vain, for the LORD will not hold him guiltless who takes his name in vain." When Moses approached God's presence, He made it clear in Exodus 3:5–6 that that He was to be feared. Then He said, "Do not come near here; remove your sandals from your feet, for the place on which you are standing is holy ground." He said also, "I am the God of your father, the God of Abraham, the God of Isaac, and the God of Jacob." Then Moses hid his face, for he was afraid to look at God. And in Psalm 29:2, it says, "Ascribe to the Lord the glory due to His name; Worship the Lord in holy array." And finally, in 2 Corinthians 10:31, it says, "So, whether you eat or drink, or whatever you do, do all to the glory of God." These and many other passages indicate that God is to be loved, respected, feared, praised, honored, and worshipped. Anything less is disrespect.

Respect for the Bible

The Bible contains the very words from God, which is why many refer to it as the "Word of God." As we read the Bible, it is literally God speaking to us. Therefore, just as we show respect for God, we must do the same for His Word. This means showing respect for the physical book, but more than that, showing respect by reading it and obeying what it says. In early history, there was no Bible, but when the first five books written by Moses became available (the Torah), they were read to the people. Consider the importance that one author placed on these books in Psalm 119:97: "Oh, how I love your law! I meditate on it all day long." And in Deuteronomy 6:6–7, we read, "God commanded Joshua as the leader of Israel, 'Do not let this Book of the Law depart from your mouth; meditate on it day and night, so that you may be careful to do everything written in it.'" God wanted His Word read (or heard) by all because it taught the people the essentials of right living and protected them from the evils of this world.

In the twenty-seven books of the New Testament, the books of the Old Testament were quoted three hundred times, illustrating just how important God's Word was to the authors. As the four Gospels and rest of the New Testament were made available, they were respectfully treated as scripture and read to the people. In 2 Timothy 3:16–17, we read, "All Scripture is breathed out by God and profitable for teaching, for reproof, for correction, and for training in righteousness, that the man of God may be complete, equipped for every good work." Scripture here refers to both the Old and New Testaments. The author of Hebrews wrote these words further illustrating the Bible's importance: "For the word of God is living and active, sharper than any two-edged sword, piercing to the division of soul and of spirit, of joints and of marrow, and discerning the thoughts and intentions of the heart" (Hebrews 4:12). The contents of the entire Bible are meant to be read, studied, meditated upon, preached from, and quoted so that we can be equipped for every good work. In doing so, we respect and honor God, the author.

Respect for Religious Leaders

In the Old Testament, it was expected that the religious leaders (e.g., priests and Levites) were afforded proper respect. They were appointed (and anointed) by God for service to the people. In New Testament times, the roles changed to elders (preachers and teachers) and deacons who were overseers of the church. In Philippians 2:29–30, Paul wrote, "Receive him (Timothy) then in the Lord with all joy, and hold men like him in high regard; because he came close to death for the work of Christ, risking his life to complete what was deficient in your service to me." And in Paul's letter to Timothy, he wrote, "The elders who rule well are to be considered worthy of double honor, especially those who work hard at preaching and teaching. For the Scripture says, 'You shall not muzzle the ox while he is threshing,' and 'The laborer is worthy of his wages'" (1 Timothy 5:17–18). The leaders were shown respect when people listened, obeyed the teachings, and supported them monetarily and physically.

Respect for Civil Authorities

The apostles Paul and Peter both gave instructions to followers of Jesus to respect civil leaders. In Romans 13:1–7, Paul gave these instructions: "Let everyone be subject to the governing authorities, for there is no authority except that which God has established. The authorities that exist have been established by God." And in 1 Titus 3:1, he said, "Remind the believers to submit to the government and its officers. They should be obedient, always ready to do what is good" (NLT). Similarly, in 1 Peter 2:13, Peter instructed us, "Submit yourselves for the LORD's sake to every human authority: whether to the emperor, as the supreme authority." And in 1 Peter 2:17, he wrote, "Show proper respect to everyone, love the family of believers, fear God, honor the emperor." In those days, just as now, some civil leaders are difficult to respect or submit to. Nevertheless, the Bible teaches that we must do this.

Respect for Parents

Obeying parents is a requirement of the fifth commandment found in Deuteronomy 5:16. It says, "Honor your father and your mother, as the

LORD your God has commanded you, so that you may live long and that it may go well with you in the land the LORD your God is giving you." Note that this command comes with a promise of benefit to those who obey. This command is repeated in the New Testament in Ephesians 6:1, "Children, obey your parents because you belong to the Lord, for this is the right thing to do" (NLT). The intent here is that children living at home must obey their parents, but also, they are expected to honor and respect their parents throughout our lives, even though as adults, the relationship has changed. Note the implication here; when we respect and honor our parents, we also respect and honor God. This does not come naturally to most children and must be taught and modeled from the beginning. Children who do not respect and obey their parents risk losing out on the promise.

Respect for Elders (Those Older)

In Middle Eastern culture, it was expected that older men and women be given proper respect. For example, the eldest of the family was given special love, honor, and respect. The elders, in turn, passed down their wisdom to the younger generations. In some Western cultures, this practice has almost disappeared. This practice was continued in the New Testament. In 1 Peter 5:5, we read, "Likewise, you younger men [of lesser rank and experience], be subject to your elders [seek their counsel]; and all of you, clothe yourselves with humility toward one another [tie on the servant's apron], for God is opposed to the proud [the disdainful, the presumptuous, and He defeats them], but He gives grace to the humble." We respect our elders by loving them, making them feel valued, listening to them, and caring for their needs.

One could easily make the case that respect should be extended to all people, regardless of position or age. After all, respect is a form of love, and Jesus commanded us to love our neighbors as ourselves (Mark 12:31). This was repeated by the apostle John in John 13:34–35, where he wrote, "A new command I give you: Love one another. As I have loved you, so you must love one another. By this all men will know that you are my disciples, if you love one another." We must then respect all people. We value them because they have been created in God's image and are special to Him.

Without respect, relationships disintegrate and can lead to all kinds of difficulty. Without respect, we end up with disrespect. This is true for families, marriages, friendships, churches, and organizations of all sizes and types. Disrespect can lead to not just disliking someone but hating them. Too, it can lead to actions that are mean-spirited and even violent. Respect, however, has the opposite effect. Respect leads to the kind of love that Jesus intended us to have for others. Moreover, it is essential for our love for God.

One can learn how to respect others as an adult, but this is not easy. Learning this as a child is far better because it can lead to a lifestyle of respect and can become incorporated naturally into one's way of thinking and behavior. Children who learn respect for their parents, God, elders, teachers, and the like will also find love and respect natural at work, in marriage, and in friendships. But children can learn disrespect at a young age too, and this is never good.

What does respect look like? It means

- obeying when asked or told;
- listening and not interrupting;
- helping and/or serving others;
- deferring decisions to elders; and
- including the opinions/ideas of others.

None of these actions are particularly hard—if we choose to love our neighbors and do not allow pride to interfere.

SELF-CONTROL

Self-control means having the ability to control one's emotions and desires, especially under difficult circumstances. Being under control in every aspect of our lives may not come easily but is surely desirable. Without self-control, we are vulnerable to all manner of things that are not good for us. Even if we achieve control in some or most areas of our lives, we remain vulnerable. Proverbs 25:28 says, "A man without self-control is like a city broken into and left without walls." This may seem like an impossible undertaking, but it is not. The Bible teaches that God does not leave us alone to fend for ourselves. Rather, He provides the help needed to overcome any challenge. In 2 Timothy 1:7, we read, "For God gave us a spirit not of fear but of power and love and self-control." When we choose to follow Jesus, the Holy Spirit teaches us how we are able to gain control over every aspect of our lives.

The Bible teaches that we especially need to have control over all things that can interfere with our relationship with God. For example, things such as food, alcohol, desires for material things, our bodies, anger, and our tongue. The concept is this: whatever may potentially have control over us, we must learn to discipline so that we have control over a particular desire or emotion. In Titus 2:11–13, we find these words: "For the grace of God has appeared that offers salvation to all people. It teaches us to say 'No' to ungodliness and worldly passions, and to live self-controlled, upright and godly lives in this present age, while we wait for the blessed hope-the appearing of the glory of our great God and Savior, Jesus Christ." And Peter admonishes us in 1 Peter 4:7, "The end of all things is at hand; therefore be self-controlled and sober-minded for the sake of your prayers." These passages instruct us *how to be* rather than providing a list of do's and don'ts.

Following are four examples of things we are to have control over.

Control over anger. James 1:19 says, "Know this, my beloved brothers: let every person be quick to hear, slow to speak, slow to anger." Proverbs 16:32 says, "Whoever is slow to anger is better than the mighty, and he who rules his spirit than he who takes a city."

Control over the tongue. Proverbs 29:11 says, "A fool gives full vent to his spirit, but a wise man quietly holds it back." Proverbs 13:3 says, "Whoever guards his mouth preserves his life; he who opens wide his lips comes to ruin."

Proverbs 18:21 says, "Death and life are in the power of the tongue, and those who love it will eat its fruits."

Control over sexual desires. First Corinthians 6:18 says, "Flee from sexual immorality. Every other sin a person commits is outside the body, but the sexually immoral person sins against his own body."

Control over alcohol consumption. Ephesians 5:18 says, "Don't be drunk with wine, because that will ruin your life. Instead, be filled with the Holy Spirit" (NLT).

The Bible assures us that we can have victory over the things that can control us. This can be quite difficult—or even impossible—to do on our own. Notice in Ephesians 5:18 the phrase "but be filled with the Spirit." This is referring to the Holy Spirit who helps us accomplish things like self-control. To be filled with the Spirit means to be led (and controlled by the Spirit). When Jesus's work on earth was finished, He promised that the Holy Spirit would be available in abundance to all who believe in Jesus. For those who follow Jesus, the Holy Spirit dwells within us. The Spirit is there to help, guide, teach, correct, remind, pray (for us), and more. For each challenge, question, or barrier, the Holy Spirit is there to guide us. There is no problem we will ever face that cannot be overcome. We can face every challenge with confidence, provided we submit our will to God and let him be in control. And with God in control, we achieve self-control. As taught in the Bible, the Holy Spirit is fully God (part of the Trinity), and so when we are filled (and led) by the Sprit, we are being led by God. In his letter to the Galatians, Paul wrote, "But the fruit of the Spirit is love, joy, peace, patience, kindness, goodness, faithfulness, gentleness, self-control" (Galatians 5:22–23). The Holy Spirit yields fruit in our lives, of which self-control is one. This is a wonderful promise and teaching found in the Bible. More can be learned about the Holy Spirit in John chapters 14 and 16. Control over our emotions and desires in all areas of our lives can be accomplished—and we are never alone in this struggle.

4

LIVING IN PEACE

And the peace of God, which transcends all understanding,
will guard your hearts and your minds in Christ Jesus.
—Philippians 4:7

One of Jesus's titles is the Prince of Peace (Isaiah 9:7), and there are many reasons for this. Jesus enables peace between us and God through His redeeming work on the cross. He suffered and died but then overcame death and now reigns over heaven and earth. As a result, we too can overcome death (spiritual) and have the assurance that we will be with Him forever in eternity. Upon Jesus's birth, the angels announced "peace on earth" to the shepherds (Luke 2:14), confirming the prophecy in Isaiah 9. Each of the topics in this chapter (hope, freedom, comfort, joy, and peace) is possible because of what Jesus did for us.

FINDING COMFORT

Comfort is a basic human want and need. There are circumstances in our lives that give rise to the need to be consoled, reassured, or calmed. For instance, there may be a personal loss, concern, change, natural disaster, conflict, misfortune, and many others. When we see someone who has needs to be comforted, our response is to find ways to comfort them—with words or actions, which sometimes may be as simple as physically being present. It should not be surprising that the Bible contains many words of comfort for every circumstance, given that its author is filled with love and compassion. Following are some of the situations along with scripture passages that provide comfort.

Comfort When Afraid

Fear is a natural reaction to things that we cannot control or that create uncertainty. But we can find comfort in knowing that we can have complete confidence in God, who is in control of all things and knows the future. The Bible teaches that we have no reason to be afraid because God is with us and for us. Consider the following passages:

> The LORD is my light and my salvation—whom shall I fear? The LORD is the stronghold of my life—of whom shall I be afraid? (Psalm 27:1)

> I sought the LORD, and He answered me, and delivered me from all my fears. (Psalm 34:4)

> When I am afraid, I put my trust in You. (Psalm 56:3)

> What then shall we say to these things? If God is for us, who is against us? (Romans 8:31 NIV)

It is good to remind ourselves that God is all-powerful. We can be assured that He has every situation under His control.

Comfort When Feeling Alone

There may be times when we are physically alone or emotionally alone. But God assures us that we are never truly alone; He is with us each hour of each day forever. And there are ways He comforts us in our aloneness. For example, He does this through scripture, through the Holy Spirit, through prayer, and by sending others to us. As stated in the Deuteronomy passage, He will never leave or forsake us.

It is the LORD who goes before you. He will be with you; he will not leave you or forsake you. Do not fear or be dismayed. (Deuteronomy 31:8)

Even though I walk through the valley of the shadow of death, I will fear no evil, for you are with me; your rod and your staff, they comfort me. (Psalm 23:4)

Comfort When Sad

The prophet Isaiah described Jesus this way in 53:3: "He was despised and rejected by men, a man of sorrows and familiar with suffering." Jesus experienced great sadness and suffering and thus can identify with times of sadness in our lives. Whenever we bring our sorrows to Him, He will provide comfort to us. He does this many ways, such as through people, circumstances, scripture, or thoughts.

He sets on high those who are lowly, and those who mourn are lifted to safety. (Job 5:11)

I have seen his ways, but I will heal him; I will lead him and restore comfort to him and to his mourners. (Isaiah 57:18)

Then the virgin will rejoice in the dance, and the young men and the old, together, for I will turn their mourning into joy, and will comfort them and give them joy for their sorrow. (Jeremiah 31:13)

Blessed are those who mourn, for they shall be comforted. (Matthew 5:4)

Comfort during Times of Trouble

Trouble comes in many forms and degrees and has a way of finding and following us all of our days. The Bible indicates that trouble is not a matter of if but when, especially for those who are obedient to Jesus. But the

Bible also provides comfort for when trouble finds us, as illustrated in the following passages:

> The Lord also will be a stronghold for the oppressed, A stronghold in times of trouble. (Psalm 9:9)

> God is our refuge and strength, a very present help in trouble. (Psalm 46:1)

> The Lord is good, A stronghold in the day of trouble, And He knows those who take refuge in Him. (Nahum 1:7)

> Blessed be God, the Father of our Lord Jesus Christ, the Father of mercies, and the God of all comfort, who comforts us in all our affliction, so that we will be able to comfort those who are in any affliction with the comfort with which we ourselves are comforted by God. (2 Corinthians 1:3–4)

> I can do all things through Him who strengthens me. (Philippians 4:13)

Comfort Regarding an Uncertain Future

Almost everyone worries about the future. We wonder about our safety, security, health, finances, employment, and the like. God understands this and admonishes us to skip the worry and simply trust Him. He knows the future and will guide us through it.

> "For I know the plans I have for you," declares the LORD, "plans to prosper you and not to harm you, plans to give you hope and a future." (Jeremiah 29:11)

> Do not be anxious about anything, but in everything by prayer and supplication with thanksgiving let your requests be made known to God. (Philippians 4:6)

And He will wipe away every tear from their eyes; and there will no longer be any death; there will no longer be any mourning, or crying, or pain; the first things have passed away. (Revelation 21:4)

What can we learn about being comforted from these scripture passages? Of this we can be certain: Jesus knows all about our troubles, our sorrows, and our cares. He not only knows that we need comfort at critical times in our lives but also knows how to comfort us. He knows exactly what we need and when. In 2 Corinthians 1:3, it says, "Blessed be the God and Father of our Lord Jesus Christ, the Father of mercies and God of all comfort." And in Isaiah 51:12, "I, even I, am He who comforts you." How does He accomplish this? God guides and directs us to scripture passages that are fit our situation, and He guides and directs people to bring comfort to us. God is able to bring the right means of comfort at the right time. Our task is to seek and trust Him.

Isaiah chapter 40:1 begins this way: "Comfort, comfort my people, says your God …" God spoke through the prophet Isaiah to His people to let them know that there were better times ahead. Their Babylonian exile was to end, and their sorrow would one day turn to joy. God did not bring immediate comfort to His people, but neither did He abandon them. In His time and His way, he assured the people that they were loved and that He had a plan. He does that for us today too. We are never abandoned and always loved, even when we may experience dark times. God has a plan of comfort for you; of that you can be certain. He delights in comforting us throughout our lives.

FINDING FREEDOM

Few words stir a stronger passion within us than does *freedom*. It is as if there is an innate desire within us to be free. To some, it means being physically free—not incarcerated and free to move about. To many others, being free means having the ability to make choices for ourselves; free to choose our career, hobbies, lifestyle, beliefs, where and how to live, how to dress, our friends, and the freedom to own property. It may also mean being free from oppression, restrictions, or even responsibilities. It is widely held that freedom is a basic human right. What is not always so clear is what we are free from and what we are free to do. For example, there are things that laws prohibit, and we are not at liberty to do or say these. And there are things we are free to do that may be harmful to us and we ought not to do.

There are two key principles about freedom that stand out in the Bible. The first is that freedom always has boundaries. People are free to make choices, but it is always God's desire that we remain within the boundaries that He sets for us. He does this because it is in our best interest to do so. God set boundaries not to restrict us but so that we could have complete freedom to operate within His moral will. The story of Adam and Eve is found in the beginning of the Bible in the book of Genesis. God had told Adam and Eve they were free to eat from any tree except one that was forbidden. This was in their best interest. They chose, however, to disobey God and eat of the forbidden fruit. Ironically, Adam and Eve's freedom of choice led to a form of bondage—to sin, which changed everything. God's boundaries were there to protect them, but sadly, they followed their own desires. Since that time, there have been numerous Bible characters whose choices were recorded; some chose to remain within the boundaries set by God, and some chose to step outside them. God established boundaries for moral living through a set of commands (e.g., do not worship other gods, honor your parents, do not lie, steal, kill, slander, covet). God did not prevent people from disobeying these and doing as they pleased, but when they did, there were consequences. King David both coveted and killed, and it cost him dearly. A man named Achan was caught stealing, and it cost him and his family their lives. The tribes of Israel chose to disobey God by worshipping idols and consequently were conquered and exiled to a foreign country. God gave broad freedoms, but when we do not follow His rules, we cause harm to both others and ourselves. A family, community, city, or nation that operates outside God's moral will (rules for living) cannot endure; it cannot succeed.

The second principle is the source of true freedom: Jesus Christ. In John 8:32, Jesus made this bold claim: "And you will know the truth, and the truth will set you free." Jesus taught that we can have freedom by knowing the truth. A few verses later (John 8:36), Jesus said, "So if the Son sets you free, you will be free indeed." True freedom really does exist, and there is a way of finding it. We often define truth as something that is factual or verifiable. But Jesus is equating truth with freedom and assures us that we can know the truth. What is this truth to which He is referring? In John 14:6, Jesus provided the answer. He was replying to a question by one of His disciples, Thomas, who asked about the way to where Jesus was going (heaven). Jesus said to him, "I am the way, and the truth, and the life. No one comes to the Father except through me." Notice what Jesus is saying here; He *is* the truth, and by knowing Him, you will find true freedom. Jesus made it clear why He came to earth—to set people free, free from the bondage of sin. Like Adam and Eve before us, we are all sinful human beings. This is abundantly clear from historical and current events. We may have freedom in the sense that we are free to make everyday choices, but without Jesus, we do not have true freedom. Jesus sets us free in that we are free from the grip that sin has on us; we are free to worship God, free to live our lives without guilt or fear, free from all worry that comes with life, and free to fulfill our purpose in life. And we live with the assurance of knowing that we will spend eternity with Jesus in heaven. We live within the boundaries that God has set for us through His commands and acknowledge that they are meant to help and protect us, not restrict us. We live within the boundaries that God set for marriage, sexuality, morality, and relationships, to mention a few. That is living in true freedom.

Many confuse freedom with self-determination, self-rule, and independence. They believe they are in control of their lives if they are free from constraints. This is based on a deep misunderstanding of freedom. If we are in control to do as we see fit but do so outside of God's boundaries, we are living and making choices without the truth. We may be autonomous but living without the one who can make us truly free. We may believe that we are free, but in reality, we are living in bondage. We become slaves to our own desires and the lies that Satan tells us. Biblical freedom means living within the boundaries that God has set for us so that we can live purpose-filled lives and be free to do what God created us to do. We are not only free from sin but are free to live our lives in victory. God gave us commands and guidelines about all aspects of our lives (as discussed elsewhere in the book), which enable us to have fulfilled lives.

One of the people set free by Jesus was the apostle Paul. How did Paul gain his freedom, and what did this mean? Prior to Paul's encounter with Jesus, he was a strict follower of all the rules and laws of the day, many of which came from man and not from God. He thought that he was doing everything right by strictly obeying them. Later, he came to realize that he had become a slave to these rules and laws. He also realized that he was a slave to sin because he could not keep God's laws perfectly. None of us can of course. Paul was a sinner in need of a savior, but then he met Jesus. Jesus saved him by extending His grace and mercy to Paul and forgiving all his sins. At that moment, Paul was set free—free from everything in his past. Paul cherished and spoke often about his freedom in Romans 8:1–2, where he explained, "There is therefore now no condemnation for those who are in Christ Jesus. For the law of the Spirit of life has set you free in Christ Jesus from the law of sin and death." Paul found the way, the truth, and the life and thereby was set free—by Jesus. Paul spent the rest of his life serving Him. He was free to choose what to eat, wear, and say and how to act. He freely chose to serve Christ to the best of his ability.

Like Paul, we are all in need of someone to set us free—truly free. In John 3:16–7, Jesus said, "For God so loved the world, that he gave his only Son, that whoever believes in him should not perish but have eternal life. For God did not send his Son into the world to condemn the world, but in order that the world might be saved through him." Jesus is that way, that truth, and that life, the one who sets us free. Finding Jesus means finding true freedom.

FINDING JOY

Joy is an emotion that occurs when we experience great pleasure or happiness. There are countless reasons why we might have joy, such as weddings, child birth, a victory, a noteworthy success, or the completion of a satisfying task. Some experience much joy in their lives, while others have little to none. But it is God's desire that we experience joy in our lives.

THE BIBLE - PRACTICAL APPLICATIONS FOR EVERYDAY LIFE

He gave us many reasons for this emotion. For example, we can find joy in His Word (Psalm 119:14), our faith (Hebrews 12:2), our identity in Him (Nehemiah 8:10), our salvation (Psalm 51:10), and even in each day that we live (Psalm 118:24). God understands very well that there are times when we experience sorrow, disappointment, and suffering. But even in these situations, there are still reasons to have joy. We will examine three specific areas in which we are to find joy.

Joy through Reading the Bible

I have experienced much joy in my life just by reading the Bible because it is filled with words of wisdom, comfort, and hope. In Psalm 119:14, the author wrote, "I rejoice in following your statutes as one rejoices in great riches." Here he was writing about God's laws and was joyful because they were like a treasure. In Jeremiah 15:16, the prophet Jeremiah wrote, "Your words were found, and I ate them, and your words became to me a joy and the delight of my heart, for I am called by your name, O LORD, God of hosts." Jeremiah "ate" (read) God's Word and was delighted because he could worship and serve none other than God Himself.

Joy in Knowing Jesus

When Jesus was born in Bethlehem, His birth was announced by angels. "But the angel said to them, "Do not be afraid. I bring you good news that will cause great joy for all the people" (Luke 2:10). Jesus's arrival meant joy for the whole world because His coming to earth meant salvation was available for all. For those who know Jesus (believe and receive Him), it means that we experience salvation and one day will be with Jesus in heaven. This is expressed by Jesus in John 17:13, where Jesus said, "But now I am coming to you, and these things I speak in the world, that they may have my joy fulfilled in themselves." And similarly, in John 15:11, Jesus said, "These things have I spoken unto you, that my joy might remain in you, and that your joy might be full." Knowing Jesus means experiencing true joy. Because of Jesus, we have hope, peace, and assurance of our salvation.

Joy from Blessings

Each and every day, we receive blessings from God, even on days that seem bad. Blessings come in all sizes and shapes, including the things we often take for granted, such as our five senses, protection, transportation, and a place to live. God wants to bless us, especially when we ask Him. In John 16:24, we read, "Until now you have asked nothing in my name. Ask, and you will receive, that your joy may be full." It is amazing that God blesses us even when we don't ask—just because He loves and cares for us. It doesn't take very long to generate a list of fifty or even a hundred blessings we receive in a single day. We can echo the words of the psalmist in Psalm 118:24, "This is the day that the LORD has made; let us rejoice and be glad in it."

Joy through Serving

Another source of joy that may seem surprising at first is serving or helping others. In John 15:11, Jesus said, "These things I have spoken to you, that my joy may be in you, and that your joy may be full." In the previous verses, Jesus had told His disciples that He would soon be leaving them but that He wanted them to experience His joy. Jesus came on earth to serve others, and He did so with joy and with love. In Mark 10:45, Jesus said, "For even the Son of Man came not to be served but to serve, and to give his life as a ransom for many." Jesus's life was all about serving others, and He not only did so joyfully, but it brought Him great joy. In John 13:15, Jesus said, "I have set you an example that you should do as I have done for you." He is our example and wants that same joy for us. By serving those in our churches, neighborhoods, communities, and beyond, we can find great joy.

Joy in Trials

The last and least likely source of joy comes with trials and even persecution. When we experience these things, we share in Jesus's own trials and suffering. In Matthew 5:11–12, Jesus said, "Blessed are you when others revile you and persecute you and utter all kinds of evil against you falsely on my account. Rejoice and be glad, for your reward is great in heaven, for so they persecuted the prophets who were before you." And in James 1:2–4, he echoed Jesus's teaching. "Count it all joy, my brothers, when you meet trials of various kinds, for you know that the testing of your faith produces steadfastness. And let steadfastness have its full effect, that you may be perfect and complete, lacking in nothing." All experiences, including unpleasant ones, can bring us joy because they help our faith to grow and because they bring rewards in heaven. Jesus will reward those who are faithful to him, even if it costs them.

In 1 Thessalonians 5:16–18, Paul wrote, "Rejoice always, pray continually, give thanks in all circumstances; for this is God's will for you in Christ Jesus." Whether we are poor or rich, healthy or sick, in prison or at home, followers of Jesus have reason to rejoice. This is because whatever our circumstances, the important thing is that we are serving Jesus. Having great wealth or status is meaningless without Christ. One day, each of us will face death. In eternity, the only things that count are those that were done for Jesus. There you will find true happiness, far greater than you could ever imagine.

Joy can be found in almost anything if we maintain a positive attitude. It is a matter of acknowledging the sources of joy and countless reasons for having a joyful heart. Joy is a combination of attitude and gratitude. We are grateful for all that God has done for us, even when things are difficult, and we live each day with a joyful heart because we live in hope.

FINDING MEANING AND PURPOSE

We find meaning in life (or purpose) through many things, such as children, careers, hobbies, wealth, status, accomplishments, pleasure, power, religion, service, or exploration. Some people can say with confidence that their lives have meaning, but sadly, many others cannot. Some even question whether life is worth living. What is it that makes life have purpose and meaning? In the Old Testament, there is a book that helps us find answers. It is called Ecclesiastes and was written by a famously wise person, King Solomon. Solomon became perhaps the wealthiest person who has ever lived. His possessions and fame were astonishing and his accomplishments remarkable. Following are several passages from 2 Chronicles chapter 9 (NIV) that describe Solomon's life:

> When the queen of Sheba heard of Solomon's fame, she came to Jerusalem to test him with hard questions. Arriving with a very great caravan—with camels carrying spices, large quantities of gold, and precious stones—she came to Solomon and talked with him about all she had on her mind. Solomon answered all her questions; nothing was too hard for him to explain to her. When the queen of Sheba saw the wisdom of Solomon, as well as the palace he had built, the food on his table, the seating of his officials, the attending servants in their robes, the cupbearers in their robes and the burnt offerings he made at the temple of the LORD, she was overwhelmed.

> Then the king made a great throne covered with ivory and overlaid with pure gold. The throne had six steps, and a footstool of gold was attached to it. On both sides of the seat were armrests, with a lion standing beside each of them. Twelve lions stood on the six steps, one at either end of each step. Nothing like it had ever been made for any other kingdom.

> King Solomon was greater in riches and wisdom than all the other kings of the earth. All the kings of the earth sought audience with Solomon to hear the wisdom God had put in his heart. Year after year, everyone who came brought a gift—articles of silver and gold, and robes, weapons and spices, and horses and mules.

> Solomon had four thousand stalls for horses and chariots, and twelve thousand horses, which he kept in the chariot cities and also with him in Jerusalem. He ruled over all

the kings from the Euphrates River to the land of the Philistines, as far as the border of Egypt. The king made silver as common in Jerusalem as stones, and cedar as plentiful as sycamore-fig trees in the foothills. Solomon's horses were imported from Egypt and from all other countries.

Later in life, King Solomon reflected on his life in the book of Ecclesiastes and came to this sad conclusion: everything that he thought would bring meaning did not; it was all meaningless. One by one, he described those things—pleasure, wealth, material possessions, social justice, food, and drink. They did not. It was not that any of these things by themselves were wrong, but these were not the goal; they were not what ultimately gave meaning to his life. Solomon pointed out that each one of us faces death—and we return to dust. We have but a short time here on earth, and then we face eternity. Then he offered this wisdom or conclusion in Ecclesiastes 12:13: "Fear God and keep His commandments, for this is the whole duty of man" (NIV). That's it! It is a simple truth and cannot be found elsewhere.

In the New Testament, the search for meaning became clearly focused on the Son, Jesus Christ. Jesus came to earth and became our personal role model, our teacher, and our Savior. He brings complete meaning and purpose to life. Meaning, then, is not found in what but in whom. It is Jesus who gives meaning to life, and we find it by focusing our lives on Him—worshipping and serving Him. Seek Him and serve Him, and you will find the answer to the question "What on earth am I here for?"

FINDING HOPE

Expressing hope is basic to human nature; we hope for things that we desire in the future. It is a feeling of expectation and desire for a certain thing to happen. We hope that what is desired can be obtained or that events will turn out the way we desire. We hope for the best, but there is some chance it may not; there is some measure of uncertainty. For example, we might hope it stops raining soon; hope to pass the test; hope our teams wins; hope to get well soon; hope everything turns out OK; hope the surgery goes well; hope to get that job; we hope and hope. But sometimes we see little reason for hope. Conflicts never seem to end, crime is widespread, natural disasters are commonplace, and many live in fear. The questions are, why should we live in hope, what is the basis of our hope, and in what do we place our hope? Hope—one little word and yet packed with meaning.

The word *hope* can be found throughout the Bible. In the Old Testament, hope is often in the context of "hoping in the Lord," "hope in God's word," or expressed in terms of confident expectation. It is frequently accompanied by the concept of trust. For example, Job, who lost everything and was even accused by his friends of committing some grievous sin, said these words about God: "Though he slay me yet will I hope in him" (Job 13:15a). Similarly, during a difficult time in his life, the prophet David ended Psalm 42 this way: "Why are you downcast O my soul? Why so disturbed within me? Put your hope in God, for I will yet praise him, for my Savior and my God." And Psalm 33:20 states, "We wait in hope for the Lord; he is our help and our shield." In the New Testament, the apostle Paul lived a life of hope in spite of numerous difficult trials. In Romans 12:12, he wrote these encouraging words: "Be joyful in hope, patient in affliction." In spite of difficult circumstances, we can be joyful in hope. These and many other scripture passages speak with great confidence about hope.

How can the Bible attach such certainty to hope? How can so many Bible characters live lives filled with hope? There is something much deeper in their hope than mere wishful thinking. You see, their hope was based on a solid foundation. To them, hope meant trusting in God's promises. God has made many promises throughout the Bible, and these are what gave them such hope. Even though these promises were not fully realized during their lifetime, they were absolutely convinced that there was something better awaiting them. So instead of hoping this or that outcome would go their way each day and year, they realized that there is more to this life, something we look forward to beyond it. And because God said it, they believed it. They put their hope in God, who has promised that no matter what happens in this life, there is something much better waiting for them. They understood that God is sovereign and in control of all things. Therefore, they trusted Him to work things out for the best—for God's purpose, not their own; they trusted God's wisdom, not theirs. This does not mean they sat back and watched life go by. Rather, they did their best at everything, working hard and living productive lives. They did this knowing that one day they would be rewarded by spending eternity in heaven. Their hope was in things that would certainly occur, but often waiting.

There is a remarkable story about three God-fearing men who were captives and servants of King Nebuchadnezzar in Babylon. They refused to bow down to an image of the king and were threatened with death by way of a furnace. They responded confidently, "O Nebuchadnezzar, we do not need to defend ourselves before you in this matter. If we are thrown into the blazing furnace, the God we serve is able to save us from it, and he will rescue us from your hand, O king. But even if he does not, we want you to know, O king, that we will not serve your gods or worship the image of gold you have set up" (Daniel 3:16–18 NIV). This short phrase "but even if He does not" spoken by the three men is stunning. The three men were not afraid of death and understood that trust and obedience to God was more important than anything else in this world. They were able to say this because of the hope they had in something better. God promises that no matter what happens in this life on earth, we will be with Him for eternity—if we put our hope and trust in Him. If God promises it, it will happen. The concerns of our daily lives are unimportant compared with eternal rewards. While uncertainty and problems come with each new day, our hope is sure. If we bring each and every one of these concerns to God in prayer, He will answer and guide us. That results in living a life of hope and confidence in the future. We are able to live lives free of fear and worry. We can share in the words of the psalmist in Psalm 119: "May those who fear you rejoice when they see me, for I have put my hope in Your Word."

There are several excellent reasons for hope, as described in the Bible. First, biblical hope is based on trust and confidence that God will do in the future what He has done in the past. In the Old Testament, we see many awesome things that God did, such as create the world, perform miracles, foretell the future, demonstrate His sovereignty over all rulers, and show His faithfulness throughout history. Jeremiah the prophet said it this way: "Nothing is too hard for God" (Jeremiah 32:17). In the New Testament, we see more amazing things done through Jesus Christ and later His apostles. In his Gospel, Mark wrote, "For all things are possible with God" (Mark 10:27). The Bible promises that God cares for people and that He is capable of doing anything. One can have complete confidence and trust in God. In Romans 15:13, He is described as the God of hope. There is no challenge in our lives too great for God, and consequently, we can live a life of hope.

Our second reason for hope is because of the saving work of Jesus Christ. Jesus came to earth, suffered, and died for the sins of the whole world. For all who put their trust in Jesus, they will be with Him forever in heaven. This gives us hope because we know that no matter what happens here on earth, we will be with Him for eternity. Heaven is what we hope for. How can one be sure that heaven is not merely wishful thinking left to chance? It is because the Bible assures those who believe that their salvation is secure. It is something that God promised in 1 John 5:11–12, "And this is the testimony: God has given us eternal life, and this life is in his Son. Whoever has the Son has life; whoever does not have the Son of God does not have life." This is truly wonderful! It is something that has already been assured. Biblical hope means that we can have complete confidence in our future, even though our current situation is difficult and we face many challenges. Hope is not baseless; it has a solid foundation.

Biblical hope has us looking beyond our lives on earth. Someday, we will all face death, but what happens then? The Bible teaches that after death, we face judgment before God. If our hope and trust are in Jesus, we can have complete confidence that we will be with Jesus forever. The alternative is unthinkable. This will certainly occur but is something for which we must wait. *Hope* in Scripture means "a strong and confident expectation." We have no reason to be afraid of the future because we know that whatever happens, we can be certain of our future. This hope is not in things on earth but in heaven. Whatever happens during our days on earth we accept with joy because we know that, good or bad, they are in God's plan. We thank God for the things that go well but also accept those things that do not. This is not our final home. There is something far better that awaits us.

The third reason for hope is because it is something that comes from God—a gift; God wants us to live hope-filled lives. Jeremiah 29:11 states, "'For I know the plans I have for you,' declares the LORD, 'plans to prosper you and not to harm you, plans to give you hope and a future'" (NIV). Even when things look dim or we grow impatient, God tells us to never lose hope. In Romans 4:18, we read, "Against all hope, Abraham in hope believed and so became the father of many nations" (NIV), and in Galatians 5:5, we read, "But by faith we eagerly await through the Spirit the righteousness for which we hope" (NIV). We wait and we hope because God said that there truly is hope. And He created us with the ability and desire to live in hope.

The Bible cautions us about placing hope in the wrong things, such as money, military strength, leaders, physical or mental abilities. These may bring temporary hope but not lasting, eternal hope. For example, in Psalm 33:17, we read, "The king is not saved by his great army; a warrior is not delivered by his great strength." And the apostle Paul put it this way in Timothy 6:17, "As for the rich in this present age, charge them not to be haughty, nor to set their hopes on the uncertainty of riches, but on God, who richly provides us with everything to enjoy." Unless our hope is based on a solid foundation, it is temporary and uncertain at best.

For some Bible characters, at times hope seemed elusive. For example, the patriarch Job felt that way after he lost everything dear to him. In Job 7:5–6, he wrote, "My flesh is clothed with worms and a crust of dirt, my skin hardens and runs. My days are swifter than a weaver's shuttle, and come to an end without hope." But of course that is not the end of the story. Job never completely lost hope, even in his darkest hour. And at the end of his book, we see the reason why; God never stopped loving and caring about Job and restored him completely.

On what then should we place our hope? The Bible explains this with great clarity in the following passages (NIV):

Hope in the Lord

But the eyes of the LORD are on those who fear him, on those whose hope is in his unfailing love, to deliver them from death and keep them alive in famine. We wait in hope for the LORD; he is our help and our shield. In him our hearts rejoice, for we trust in his holy name. May your unfailing love rest upon us, O LORD, even as we put our hope in you. (Psalm 33:118–22)

I wait for the LORD, my soul waits, and in his word I put my hope. My soul waits for the Lord more than watchmen wait for the morning, more than watchmen wait for the morning. O Israel, put your hope in the LORD, for with the LORD is unfailing love and with him is full redemption. He himself will redeem Israel from all their sins. (Psalm 130:5–8)

Hope in God's Promises

And now it is because of my hope in what God has promised our fathers that I am on trial today. This is the promise our twelve tribes are hoping to see fulfilled as they earnestly serve God day and night. O king, it is because of this hope that the Jews are accusing me. (Acts 26:6–7)

And again, Isaiah says, "The Root of Jesse will spring up, one who will arise to rule over the nations; the Gentiles will hope in him." May the God of hope fill you with all joy and peace as you trust in him, so that you may overflow with hope by the power of the Holy Spirit. (Romans 15:12–13)

Hope in Our Salvation

Therefore, since we have been justified through faith, we have peace with God through our Lord Jesus Christ, through whom we have gained access by faith into this grace in which we now stand. And we rejoice in the hope of the glory of God. Not only so, but we also rejoice in our sufferings, because we know that suffering produces perseverance; perseverance, character; and character, hope. And hope does not disappoint us, because God has poured out his love into our hearts by the Holy Spirit, whom he has given us. (Romans 5:1–5)

Hope in Christ

But in your hearts set apart Christ as Lord. Always be prepared to give an answer to everyone who asks you to give the reason for the hope that you have. But do this with gentleness and respect, keeping a clear conscience, so that those who speak maliciously against your good behavior in Christ may be ashamed of their slander. (1 Peter 3:13–14)

Ours then should be hope-filled lives, hope-filled families, and hope-filled communities in a hope-filled world.

FINDING PEACE

It is likely that we have all experienced what it is like to be without peace even though most, if not all, of us have an innate desire to be at peace. We want an inner peace in our relationships and in our work and home environments, with family members, friends, and neighbors, and with ourselves. Too, we long for peace within our communities, countries, and our world. News of peace is something that is pleasant to our ears. Consider a person about to face the most difficult challenge they have ever faced. They might very well experience anxiety to the point that it affects all aspects of their life. But instead, this person feels completely at ease; all anxiety and fears have evaporated. She feels an incredible sense of peace, no matter the outcome, and feels completely confident about her future. How and why might this person have such inner peace? And how might we find peace in a world that has so little of it?

The concept of peace in the Bible comes from the word *shalom*. Although it has a range of meanings, it generally means well-being. It was used during greetings, such as "Peace to you." It was also used to designate relationships between individuals, groups, or nations, or simply the absence of hostility. It also referred to situations, such as living in peace, economic prosperity, or security. For example, in Leviticus 26:6, it says, "I will grant peace in the land and you will lie down and no one will make you afraid." And in Romans 9:22, we are instructed to live at peace with our neighbors; "If it is possible, as far as it depends on you, live at peace with everyone." In addition to peace between people, it can also mean peace of mind, the inner peace or tranquility in our souls, something that is wonderful though difficult to describe. The word *peace* occurs in nearly every book of the Bible and more than two hundred times overall. Following are several ways that the Bible instructs us about living at peace.

Seek the God of Peace

The best way to become a peacemaker is to see God who values peace. In the following passages, the apostle Paul uses these words to describe God:

> May the God of peace be with you all. Amen. (Romans 15:33)

> And the peace of God, which surpasses all understanding, will guard your hearts and your minds in Christ Jesus. (Philippians 4:7)

> And the God of peace will be with you. (Philippians 4:9)

> Now may the God of peace himself sanctify you completely.
> May your entire spirit, soul and body be kept blameless at
> the coming of our Lord Jesus Christ. (1 Thessalonians 5:23)

In these passages, we see that peace is a part of the very nature of God. In many other passages, peace is something that comes from God as a blessing. For example, in Psalm 29:11, we read, "The Lord gives strength to his people; the Lord blesses his people with peace." God understands and desires peace for us. By bringing our challenges and worries to Him, we can find true and lasting peace.

Find Inner Peace through Jesus Christ

True and lasting peace is possible, and it is available to anyone. It is found in the person of Jesus Christ. In Isaiah 9:6, Jesus is described as the Prince of Peace, and in Luke 2:14, Jesus's birth is announced as bringing peace on earth. And in John 14:27, Jesus said, "Peace I leave with you, my peace I give you. Not as the world gives do I give to you. Let not your hearts be troubled, neither let them be afraid." This is a wonderful peace that comes by believing in and trusting Jesus. It is not the kind of peace that is found through money, education, power, status, or anything else. The death and resurrection of Jesus makes peace possible between God and man. As a result, we have peace in our hearts—the kind of peace that the world cannot understand. This is reinforced in John 16:33, where it says, "I have told you these things, so that in me you may have peace. In this world you will have trouble. But take heart! I have overcome the world."

The apostle Paul explained the wonderful peace we can experience in Romans 5:1, where it says, "Therefore, since we have been justified through faith, we have peace with God through our Lord Jesus Christ." Now that is a wonderful thought, isn't it? We can be at peace with God because of what Jesus has done for us. That brings genuine and lasting peace in our hearts. We have nothing to fear in this world. Then in Colossians 3:15, Paul also wrote, "Let the peace of Christ rule in your hearts, which indeed you were called in one body. And be thankful." Further, in Philippians 4:7, Paul wrote, "And the peace of God which surpasses all understanding, will guard your hearts and your minds in Christ Jesus." We can have peace in our hearts even though there may be trouble all around us—sickness, hunger, opposition, uncertainty. We can be at peace. Jesus wants to be our friend, and all it takes for this is to believe in and put your trust in Him. The door is always open to talk with Him. He listens carefully to everything we say and deeply wants to help us overcome every challenge we face. A friend like that is hard to find here on earth but not in heaven.

Be a Peacemaker

Not only can we find peace in our lives, but we can help others find it as well. The Bible teaches that we should be peacemakers, seeking unity and harmony with others. The following passages illustrate this teaching:

> Better a dry crust with peace and quiet than a house full of feasting, with strife. (Proverbs 17:1 NIV)

> Blessed are the peacemakers, for they will be called sons of God. (Matthew 5:9)

> So then let us pursue what make for peace and mutual upbuilding. (Romans 14:19)

> Strive for peace with everyone, and for the holiness without which no one will see the Lord. (Hebrews 12:14)

> But the wisdom from above is first pure, then peaceable, gentle, open to reason, full of mercy and good fruits, impartial and sincere. (James 3:17)

In these passages, we see that peace is something that we work at and strive for in our lives. Making peace encourages and builds up others. The opposite of a peacemaker is someone who creates trouble and disunity and tears down; this is most displeasing to God. Note the blessing that comes to those who make peace. Also note in the James passage the parallel words that accompany making peace. This provides guidance as to how we are to become peacemakers, whether at home, at work, in our community, or between nations. These virtues do not come naturally to many of us and is the reason why making peace requires effort and diligence.

Peace is a wonderful blessing that God promises because of His great love for you and me. In Psalm 29:11, it says, "May the Lord give strength to his people; May the Lord bless his people with peace." God blesses individuals, families, communities, and even nations with peace, provided they put their trust in Him. The peace we find described in the Bible can overcome fear, anxiety, anger, and so much more. If you cannot find peace, it is most likely because you are not searching in the right place. Seek the God of peace through prayer and reading the Bible; then you will discover lasting peace.

PREVENTING INTERPERSONAL CONFLICT

When individuals or groups disagree or oppose each other, especially if serious in nature, we describe this as conflict. Generally, we think of conflict in negative terms because it represents disharmony between individuals or groups. We much prefer unity and harmony and agreement. Conflict may be benign, or it can escalate into arguing, shouting, physical contact, and more. Once there is conflict, the Bible has much to say about resolving it—more than space permits here. But it also has excellent guidance on the prevention of conflict, which we will examine here.

While it is impossible to avoid all conflict, it is possible to live a peace-filled life. The author of Hebrews provided this wisdom: "Strive for peace with everyone, and for the holiness without which no one will see the Lord" (Hebrews 12:14). It is true that not all conflict is bad; some may even be helpful, which we will cover later. There are words and actions that seem to encourage conflict. But the Bible contains wisdom that helps us prevent it, especially the type of conflict that escalates and can cause damage. Below are six things that help us achieve a life of peace.

Be a Good Listener

In Proverbs 18:13, it says, "If one gives an answer before he hears, it is his folly and shame." Sometimes we are so eager to express our thoughts that we fail to listen to others. Or we may pretend we are listening while planning our response. The intent here is to listen to gain a good understanding of others. To do otherwise is folly and shame because we show disrespect and a lack of judgment. We are often anxious to have our own ideas heard because we believe them to be better than those of others. But if not controlled, it can lead to anger and conflict. Proverbs 21:23 says, "Whoever keeps his mouth and his tongue keeps himself out of trouble." Speaking without hearing is likely to bring trouble." And James 1:19–21 says, "Know this, my beloved brothers: let every person be quick to hear, slow to speak, slow to anger; for the anger of man does not produce the righteousness of God." James makes it abundantly clear that to be right with God, we must be good listeners and choose our words wisely. Poor listening skills combined with words that inflame leads to anger both for the speaker and listener. This accomplishes nothing and is not honoring to God.

Give a Gentle Answer

Proverbs 15:1 provides excellent advice for us. "A soft answer turns away wrath, but a harsh word stirs up anger." Some translations use the term *gentle answer.* Harsh words all too easily flow from our mouths and often lead toward a war of words or worse. Gentle answers may be difficult for us but demonstrate wisdom and self-control. Nothing is to be gained by harsh words, but gentle answers can lead to understanding and peace.

Do Not Argue

Another way we can avoid conflict is to simply choose to not argue. Proverbs 17:14 provides this wisdom: "The beginning of strife is like letting out water, so quit before the quarrel breaks out." Imagine an earthen dam that has sprung a small leak. If caught early, the water can be contained and repaired. But if allowed to continue, it can lead to great destruction. Once a discussion transitions into an argument, it too can lead to an undesirable outcome. Many a broken relationship has resulted from a small quarrel.

Never Seek Revenge

Revenge can cause or escalates conflict. Romans 12:17–19 says, "Repay no one evil for evil, but give thought to do what is honorable in the sight of all. If possible, so far as it depends on you, live peaceably with all. Beloved, never avenge yourselves, but leave it to the wrath of God, for it is written, "Vengeance is mine, I will repay, says the Lord." It is never up to us to repay someone for what they said or did. Many Bible passages instruct us to forgive and let the matter go. God knows whether we were wronged, and in His infinite wisdom and perfect timing, He will determine if, how, and when punishment should occur.

Always Be Honest

Often, conflict can be prevented by simply being honest. Proverbs 16:28 says, "A dishonest man spreads strife, and a whisperer separates close friends." We must choose to be honest with our words by never saying things that are untrue, mean, or harmful. Similarly, our actions must not be dishonest. When our words or actions are dishonest, it often results in others being offended, angry, or hateful, and conflict is one of the natural outcomes. Strive for 100 percent honesty.

Seek God's Wisdom

In all situations, seek God's wisdom. As mentioned earlier, Proverbs 3:5–6 provides this excellent advice: "Trust in the Lord with all your heart, and do not lean on your own understanding. In all your ways acknowledge him, and he will make straight your paths." Trust God to guide you in all matters. He will never grow tired of listening to you and delights in helping you in any situation, regardless of how big or small it is. Our own understanding is always limited, but His is not. Another translation puts it this way: "And He will direct your paths." This is a wonderful promise. Imagine the God of the universe giving you personal guidance so that you will succeed. In Romans 12:18, the apostle Paul offered this advice: "If possible, so far as it depends on you, live peaceably with all." Conflict, the kind that should be avoided, can be prevented if we choose to lean on God's understanding rather than our own.

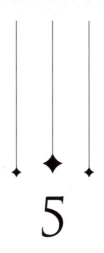

5

SUCCESSFUL RELATIONSHIPS

Above all, love each other deeply, because love
covers over a multitude of sins.
—1 Peter 4:8

How we relate to others can make all the difference in our lives. On the positive side, relationships can be described with words such as strong, good, friendly, warm, loving, helpful, enjoyable, fun, or lasting. On the negative side, we might use words like distant, strained, hurtful, stressful, abusive, broken, or even hateful. It would seem intuitive that everyone would strive toward positive relationships, but all too often, relationships either begin or end up on the negative side. Positive relationships sometimes come easily and naturally but also can require a great deal of effort. The expression *relationship building* is often appropriate to capture the amount of effort required to make it positive. And to change a relationship from negative to positive may necessitate extraordinary effort. The Bible has much to say about relationships because we are designed to live our lives surrounded by people with whom we interact. It offers great wisdom about how to develop and maintain positive ones and prevent the negative.

FRIENDSHIP

Everyone needs a friend. Friendship is one of the most important relationships in life—people to talk to, do things with, to love and be loved, provide help, share joy with, and so much more. We were designed to flourish in community with others, including friends. Some friendships are short lived, while others can last a lifetime. Friendships can even provide meaning and purpose. Those who have no friends truly miss out.

There are many principles of friendship taught directly in scripture passages or indirectly through examples. We will examine twelve of these here.

Choose your friends wisely. The Bible admonishes us to be careful with whom we closely associate. This is evident from the following scripture passages (NIV):

> The righteous choose their friends carefully, but the way of the wicked leads them astray. (Proverbs 12:26)

> Walk with the wise and become wise, for a companion of fools suffers harm. (Proverbs 13:20)

> One who has unreliable friends soon comes to ruin, but there is a friend who sticks closer than a brother. (Proverbs 18:24)

> Do not make friends with a hot-tempered person, do not associate with one easily angered, or you may learn their ways and get yourself ensnared. (Proverbs 22:24–25)

> Do not be misled: Bad company corrupts good character. (1 Corinthians 15:33)

We can have an influence on others, but they also can influence us, and this may be for better or for worse. Having the right (or wrong) friends makes all the difference. It usually does not take very long to tell whether someone fits the description of "bad company," "unreliable," or "hot tempered," as mentioned above. This does not mean that we must shun these people, but the Bible indicates that we should not be in close fellowship with them so that they influence us for the worse.

Friends help and support one another. We see this in Ecclesiastes 4:9–12 where it says, "Two are better than one, because they have a good return for their labor: If either of them falls down, one can help the other up. But pity anyone who falls and has no one to help them up. Also, if two lie down together, they will keep warm. But how can one keep warm alone? Though one may be overpowered, two can defend themselves. A cord of three strands is not quickly broken." Friends can help us make wise decisions, avoid mistakes, encourage us, pray for us, comfort us, and help us through life. They are like a precious gift that blesses, enriches, and helps us grow and flourish.

Friends provide trustworthy advice. We all need advice at times, sometimes daily. Where can we find good advice? Proverbs 27:9 says, "Oil and perfume make the heart glad, and the sweetness of a friend comes from his earnest counsel." A friend provides wise counsel that seeks to be in one's best interest. It is offered from the heart out of genuine love. Bad advice leads us down the wrong path and results in dangerous or destructive decisions. For instance, prisons are full of people who have followed bad advice. But if someone is a friend, they steer us away from things that will harm us. A trusted friend can make our heart glad.

Friends stand by each other during difficult times. Many of us (including the author) have found ourselves mired in a pit. A friend not only helps us avoid life's pits, but once in a pit, they help us escape. In Proverbs 17:17, we read, "A friend loves at all times, and a brother is born for a time of adversity." Daniel chapter 1 is the story about Daniel and three friends who were captives in a foreign country and were faced the difficult (and dangerous) decision to reject the offer to eat food at the king's table, specially prepared for them. They stood firm together and chose to trust God and not defile themselves with food offered to a pagan god. They stood by one another and faced a desperate situation together.

Friends are present for each other. There is a great passage in the book of Job that describes Job's friends coming to comfort Job after his overwhelming disaster. Job 2:11 says, "When Job's three friends, Eliphaz the Temanite, Bildad the Shuhite and Zophar the Naamathite, heard about all the troubles that had come upon him, they set out from their homes and met together by agreement to go and sympathize with him and comfort him." Job's friends sat with him an entire week before any of them spoke a word. Often, simply being present or listening is all that is needed to carry us through the valleys of life.

Friends are honest with each other. We see this in Proverbs 27:5–6 where it says, "Better is open rebuke than hidden love. Wounds from a friend can be trusted, but an enemy multiplies kisses." It all begins with honesty and genuine love for another human being. Sometimes friends are brutally honest to the point that it may hurt deeply. But true friends say and do things that may sting for a reason. It is because what they say or do is in the best interest of their friends and because they love their friends. And it is because they would trust that the friend would do the same for them. Often, others can see things that we cannot and steer us away from things that may harm us. In so doing, friends help each other become stronger as individuals.

Friends encourage one another. There is a wonderful verse in Proverbs 27:17 that says, "As iron sharpens iron, so one person sharpens another." True friends help each other grow and learn from experiences by speaking the truth in love, being encouraging, protecting, and bringing out the best in others. For instance, all of us make mistakes at times. A friend (in a loving and kind way) can help us learn from those mistakes and avoid the same or similar mistake. In 1 Thessalonians 5:11, the apostle Paul said, "Therefore encourage one another and build each other up." As we encourage and guide our friends toward the truth found in the Bible, we grow stronger together.

We encourage friends by doing or saying things that inspire and give them confidence. The apostle Paul's life was characterized by the encouragement of others. As we read Paul's letters to the churches, we notice that they contain many words of encouragement (e.g., 1 and 2 Timothy). He wrote and spoke with love and concern for others, which gave them courage and hope. Paul also mentioned that he too was encouraged by others—by their words and their actions, such as their faith, giving, support, and prayers.

Friends follow Jesus's golden rule. This was taught by Jesus in Luke 6:31, where He said, "Do to others as you would have them do to you." Friends treat others as they would like to be treated. For example, if we want to be respected, we treat others with respect. If we want to be loved, we show our love to our friends. If we want to be forgiven, we must forgive others.

Friends are faithful to each other. Before he became king, David developed a strong friendship with King Saul's son Jonathan (1 Samuel 18:1–4, 20:1–42). Jonathan demonstrated great loyalty to David by warning him about his father's plot to kill David. After he became king, David demonstrated his loyalty to Jonathan by showing kindness to one of Jonathan's crippled sons. A good friend will not be deterred by difficult circumstances, nor will they abandon their companions. Things can become complicated and difficult at times, even frightening, but true friends remain faithful through the low points.

Friends forgive each other. Sooner or later, all friends make mistakes; they say or do things that are offensive. But this should not cause the end of the friendship. Rather, friends learn to forgive each other. In fact, they never stop forgiving each other. In Ephesians 4:32, it says, "Be kind to one another, tenderhearted, forgiving one another, as God in Christ forgave you." Just as Jesus forgives us, we forgive others. When we forgive the mistakes of our friends, we are demonstrating our love for Jesus, who wants us to do this very thing. And as we forgive, we enable good friendships to deepen and grow stronger. In so doing, we help develop our own character as well as that of the friend.

Friends love one another. Love is another critically important element of friendship. The things friends say and do for each other are motivated by love. In John 15:12, Jesus said, "My command is this: Love each other as I have loved you." Jesus understood how difficult it is for us to love other people, even friends. Our tendency is to love ourselves much more than others. Some people, including close friends, can be quite difficult to love at times. Nevertheless, we are to love our friends as Christ loves us, unconditionally.

We see love on display in the person of Jesus Christ. Jesus and His disciples had been together almost constantly for three years, and Jesus knew them intimately. Jesus not only knew His disciples perfectly, but He also knew their future. He knew that they would make mistakes, say things that demonstrated their lack of understanding, and even desert Him.

There is one more important aspect of friendship, one that is profound and astonishing. God desires to be friends with us. In spite of our weaknesses and mistakes, God seeks to have fellowship with us. Near the end of Jesus's ministry, he called His disciples friends (John 15:15). He said this because he desires a personal relationship with us. And then Jesus demonstrated just how serious He was about this friendship by doing something most extraordinary—He suffered and died for them. He made the supreme sacrifice for His disciples (friends)—because of His deep love for them. He also forgave them completely for everything they ever did (or would do) wrong. Jesus did that for each one of us too. He is your friend and my friend, in spite of the mistakes we make. Jesus is a forever friend who loves us more than we can ever imagine. Jesus's love for His followers today is no different from that of His disciples. He gave His life for them and for anyone else who puts their faith and trust in Him. Jesus's example teaches us that genuine friendship means loving one another unconditionally, forgiving one another, accepting one another, and serving one another.

Each Bible character in the examples above had this in common: they all loved and served God. Their love and caring for others was grounded in their love for and service to God. God was not only involved in their friendships but became the foundation. They understood that their love for God and service to Him was what brought them together and that it was God who gave them strength and courage. That is the case for us too.

Friendships that are based on a solid foundation will thrive. And following these principles helps us keep our relationships positive.

MARRIAGE

There are advantages to being single, as exemplified by Paul, such as being fully available to serve others. Whether single or married, one can live a fulfilled life of service to God and community. Scripture does not say that everyone should get married, only that those who do must comprehend the meaning and importance of marriage. The apostle Paul taught that marriage is not for everyone (1 Corinthians 7). For those who do choose to marry, the Bible provides the essential guidelines that two married people should abide by and respect. The Bible's teachings on marriage emphasize three key principles: God's design for marriage, God's desire for marriage, and the principles for staying married.

God's Design for Marriage

From the beginning, marriage was a part of God's plan for men and women. It was God's design to have man and woman together as husband and wife, as occurred with Adam and Eve. In Genesis 2:18, we read, "The LORD God said, 'It is not good for the man to be alone. I will make a helper suitable for him.'" Adam and Eve were to live, raise children, and experience all that life offered—together. They were united as one, man and woman, husband and wife. In Genesis 2:24, we read, "Therefore a man shall leave his father and his mother and hold fast to his wife, and they shall become one flesh." One flesh means that they were to be united emotionally and physically. God designed us this way because marriage provides the best environment for children to be born (or adopted). The father and mother provide, teach, and train them in preparation for life, including preparation to love and serve God throughout their lives.

God's Desire for Marriage

God intended that a husband and wife unite together and then become as one, being fully committed to each other throughout their lives. This is because marriage is a covenant commitment between two people (Malachi 2:14). And this commitment is not only to each other but also with God. In Matthew 19:6, Jesus said, "What God has joined together, let no one separate." Separation is not included in God's design for marriage. And in Hebrews 13:14, it says, "Let marriage be held in honor among all, and let the marriage bed be undefiled, for God will judge the sexually immoral and adulterous." God's desire was that once two people were united in marriage, they were to remain faithful to each other and remain so until death. He expressed His views on this in the strongest of terms.

Early on in history, God's intent for marriage gave way to human desires resulting in a breakdown of marriage. Physical relationships outside of marriage, divorce, and prostitution entered the scene. These practices were detestable to God. In the New Testament, Jesus answered a question about divorce in Mark 10:1–9.

> Some Pharisees came and tested him by asking, "Is it lawful for a man to divorce his wife?" "What did Moses command you?" he replied. They said, "Moses permitted a man to write a certificate of divorce and send her away." It was because your hearts were hard that Moses wrote you this law," Jesus replied. "But at the beginning of creation God made them male and female. For this reason a man will leave his father and mother and be united to his wife, and the two will become one flesh. So they are no longer two, but one flesh. Therefore what God has joined together, let no one separate."

Note what Jesus said about the cause of divorce: "your hearts were hard." Hard hearts means that they are unloving, proud, selfish, and calloused; they were not open to learning and being taught what is right in God's eyes. The people did not follow God's commands. They did what they thought was right in their own eyes rather than God's. Hard hearts destroy marriages. And from the Old Testament book of Malachi 2:16, we find these words: "'For I hate divorce!' says the LORD, the God of Israel. 'To divorce your wife is to overwhelm her with cruelty,' says the LORD of Heaven's Armies. 'So guard your heart; do not be unfaithful to your wife'" (NLT).

The Bible passages on marriage may be difficult for us to accept. Like the people in ancient times, our hearts tend to be hard too. We take marriage lightly, and divorce has become commonplace in some societies. Nevertheless, God's way is always the best way.

Principles for Staying Married

The relationship between husband and wife is intended to be characterized by genuine and lasting love. Jesus commanded us to love one another (John 13:34–25), and this, of course, applies to husbands and wives. In Ephesians 5:25, the apostle Paul reinforced this teaching: "Husbands, love your wives, as Christ loved the church and gave himself up for her." And in Ephesians 5:28, Paul continues, "In the same way husbands should love their wives as their own bodies. He who loves his wife loves himself." Jesus loves us so much that He gave His own life for us. He did everything possible so that we can have freedom from sin. In the same way, a husband must love his wife by giving himself up for her. He must be loving, kind, fully committed, and forgiving. These words also apply to the wife, who must love and respect her husband in all that she says and does. Husbands and wives make mistakes, sometimes often. The advice offered in 1 Peter 4:8 is the perfect remedy for mistakes. "Above all, keep loving one another earnestly, since love covers a multitude of sins." We are to love others in spite of these sins. Husbands and wives who love each other as described in the Bible fulfill God's purpose for marriage, and this pleases God.

The apostle Paul described the kind of love that should exist within marriage exceptionally well in 1 Corinthians 13:4–8. "Love is patient and kind; love does not envy or boast; it is not arrogant or rude. It does not insist on its own way; it is not irritable or resentful; it does not rejoice at wrongdoing, but rejoices with the truth. Love bears all things, believes all things, hopes all things, and endures all things. Love never ends." This is the kind of love that Jesus wants and expects in a marriage. Husbands and wives who follow this teaching will have a successful marriage.

Genuine love also involves forgiving one another. Jesus also taught that we should forgive continuously (Luke 17:3–4; Ephesians 4:32). A spouse may do or say something that is deeply hurtful or offensive and seemingly unforgivable. Nevertheless, Jesus expects us to forgive the spouse just as He forgives things we do that are deeply hurtful or offensive to Him and are seemingly unforgivable. Forgiveness is difficult and may require great effort (and courage). But forgive we must, and for some, this means doing so often, even daily. We are required to forgive one another just as Jesus forgave and continues to forgive us.

Another principle for making the marriage a lasting one is to put Christ first in the marriage. The Bible teaches us that husbands and wives must seek to be Christlike in all that they do (1 Corinthians 11:1). The husband and wife submit to Jesus's teachings and obey all His commands. They seek God's purposes for their lives, not their own. Their thoughts, words, and actions are guided by the Holy Spirit (sent to us by Jesus), who leads, guides, teaches, convicts, helps, reminds, strengthens, and comforts us at all times in all situations. They seek not their own will but God's will to be done. Putting Christ first means resisting temptation. Jesus provided an excellent example of how this is done. In Mark chapter 1, we find the story about Jesus's temptation by Satan. Despite being promised many things by Satan, Jesus rebukes him with scripture. Jesus experienced intense temptation and understands those we face as humans. Moreover, Jesus is always there to help us overcome each one. In Hebrews 2:18, the author wrote, "For because he himself has suffered when tempted, he is able to help those who are being tempted." Jesus is always there to help us. These temptations come from our internal desires, as pointed out by a leader in the early church. In James 1:14–16, we find "But each person is tempted when he is lured and enticed by his own desire. Then desire when it has conceived gives birth to sin, and sin when it is fully grown brings forth death. Do not be deceived, my beloved brothers." Temptations of all kinds affect husbands and wives, but every one of these can be overcome if we keep our focus on Jesus. In 1 Corinthians 10:13, the apostle Paul wrote,

"No temptation has overtaken you that is not common to man. God is faithful, and he will not let you be tempted beyond your ability, but with the temptation he will also provide the way of escape, that you may be able to endure it." Help is always on the way—if we seek it.

Putting Christ first also means recognizing and overcoming the enemy of marriage, Satan. Satan hates marriage, and he will do anything within his power to deceive and destroy it. In 2 Corinthians 2:11, the apostle Paul wrote, "So that we would not be outwitted by Satan; for we are not ignorant of his designs." Satan will attempt to deceive a husband or wife into believing lies or half-truths about themselves, the spouse, and so on. But all attempts by Satan can be overcome by doing these things: reading the Bible, prayer, maintaining a focus on Jesus, and remaining in fellowship with other believers. Pray for your marriage regularly. If possible, pray with your spouse. God will guide you through even the most difficult of circumstances when you do. Satan is not all-powerful; only Jesus is, and Jesus will help us defeat Satan if we invite Him to do so.

When sin entered the world, many things changed, including marriage. Things such as lying, unfaithfulness, deceit, and physical and emotional abuse entered the husband-wife relationship, resulting in broken marriages and divorce. Today, all these same issues are present. Plus we have a new set of distractions and temptations. Our broken world has resulted in many broken marriages and children being raised in far less than ideal situations. But God's design for marriage has not changed. Marriage between a man and woman was and remains the standard. More than ever, we need to understand God's design for marriage and need God's help daily in protecting our marriage. If you have not done so, invite God into your marriage; you will be greatly blessed.

PARENTING

Raising children can be both one of the most difficult and one of the most rewarding tasks that adults face. Children can tax our patience like nothing else and push us to our limits. But they can also bring great joy and blessings in ways that are hard to capture with words. In Psalm

127:3–5, it says, "Behold, children are a heritage from the Lord, the fruit of the womb, a reward. Like arrows in the hand of a warrior are the children of one's youth. Blessed is the man who fills his quiver with them!" It brings great satisfaction to fathers and mothers to see their children grow and mature into adults and accomplish many things during their lives. But it requires hard work and perseverance to successfully launch a child into adulthood. And it requires wisdom to guide children down the right path. The Bible provides some excellent guidance about how this should be done by emphasizing two key actions—teaching and correcting.

Teaching

The teaching the Bible refers to is not the typical subjects, such as reading and math. Rather, they are the things that lead to moral living and love for God. In the book of Deuteronomy, we find several passages that emphasize the importance of teaching children.

> Only be careful and watch yourselves closely so that you do not forget the things your eyes have seen or let them slip from your heart as long as you live. Teach them to your children and their children after them. (Deuteronomy 4:9 NIV)

> And these words that I command you today shall be on your heart. You shall teach them diligently to your children, and shall talk of them when you sit in your house, and when you walk by the way, and when you lie down, and when you rise. (Deuteronomy 6:6–7)

> You shall teach them to your children, talking of them when you are sitting in your house, and when you are walking by the way, and when you lie down, and when you rise. (Deuteronomy 11:19)

In these Deuteronomy passages, Moses was referring to God's commandments and the mighty acts that the people saw God do. These verses are not mere suggestions; they are warnings and commands. God reminded the adults many times to teach their children what He had taught them. Why did He do this? It is because many parents fail to teach the lessons they themselves learned from their parents. Perhaps they forgot them, became too busy, or simply underestimated the importance. No matter the reason, parents must take responsibility for their children's education, even though it may be other adults who do the teaching. Note here what God wanted the children to learn; it is the moral law that God gave to the people (i.e., the Ten Commandments). Parents who fail to impress these upon their children run the risk of sons and daughters who have no moral grounding. They may even drift away from God altogether. We see this very thing happening in the book of Judges and later in the books of 1 and 2 Kings. Over and over, the people drifted away from God, repented, and returned to God only to repeat the process. Sadly, we have seen this occurring in all cultures and societies since that time.

God not only commanded us to teach our children but also provided us with this promise found in Isaiah 54:13: "All your children shall be taught by the LORD, and great shall be the peace of your children." The well-being of children is tied directly to their knowledge of God—and of course their faithfulness to God. That is an amazing promise and a convincing reason to teach children about God and all the things that God desires that we know. Proverbs 22:6 says, "Train up a child in the way he should go; even when he is old he will not depart from it." Instruct them about who God is, what great things He has done, who they belong to (they are children of God), and respect for God's commands. Note that the word "train" is used here. This implies not only imparting knowledge but the practical application of how to worship and obey God. A great example of this is found in Timothy, who became a significant leader in the church. This was captured in 2 Timothy 3:14–15 where it says, "But as for you, continue in what you have learned and have been convinced of, because you know those from whom you learned it, and how from infancy you have known the Holy Scriptures which are able to make you wise for salvation through faith in Christ Jesus." Timothy was taught by his mother and grandmother, and the lessons that he learned as a child were applied throughout his adult life. Although not specifically mentioned, all Old

Testament leaders, such as Abraham, Isaac, and Jacob, learned from their parents and other teachers, and this instruction served them well through their lives, just as God had promised.

Because parents are responsible for their children's moral education, it follows that they themselves must understand God's moral laws well enough to be able to teach them. Moreover, they must necessarily believe them and put them into practice. Otherwise, what they teach has no substance. Children notice those things.

Correcting

The second emphasis in scripture is for parents to discipline or correct their children. Discipline is critical for the development of a child for many reasons. Consider these proverbs:

> To discipline a child produces wisdom, but a mother is disgraced by an undisciplined child. (Proverbs 29:15–17 NLT)

> Discipline your children, and they will give you peace of mind and will make your heart glad. (Proverbs 29:17)

> Those who spare the rod of discipline hate their children. Those who love their children care enough to discipline them. (Proverbs 13:24)

Correction, or discipline, leads to wisdom because it enables the learning process. A child learns right from wrong, the importance of making good choices, and how to respect others. Too, as the child matures into adulthood, they are able to understand their relationship to God and obeying Him, as He is in authority over them. Children who disobey their parents will likely also disobey God, both of which are most unfortunate. The former brings disgrace to parents and the latter separation from God. But a son or daughter who is corrected as needed brings joy and comfort. Parents who do not discipline their children are doing a great disservice to them. The Bible uses strong language here, "hate," but that is to contrast this with the genuine love that comes with discipline. The use of the term *rod* is a figure of speech and does not imply or advocate striking a child. Rods were used for herding and guiding sheep in the direction that the shepherd desired and for protection of the flock. A wise and loving parent guides, directs, and corrects their children so that they will become successful in life and wise parents themselves. Discipline guides a child away from behaviors that can be destructive and dangerous and toward right living.

The Bible mentions a number of parents who were not exemplary in leadership at home. There is a sad example in 1 Samuel 2:12–17 of a priest named Eli who failed to discipline his two sons, and this resulted in shameful behavior, defilement of the temple in which they served. Eli did not confront or correct them, which contributed to a tragic end to all three. In the end, they were all severely punished. In Ephesians 6:4, the apostle Paul made this statement: "Fathers, do not provoke your children to anger, but bring them up in the discipline and instruction of the Lord." How might a father provoke a child to anger? It is by being unfair, disciplining without love, being harsh, being critical, or disciplining in anger. Parents also make the mistake playing favorites—loving one child more than another. These things are harmful to children and displeasing to God. Isaac and Rebecca played favorites with their two sons, and that caused friction within the family. And the patriarch Jacob had favorite sons, which also led to friction and even hatred among the twelve brothers.

The Child's Role

Children also have responsibilities, especially as they grow older. The fifth of the Ten Commandments states, "Honor your father and mother, so that you may live long in the land the Lord your God is giving you" (Exodus 20:12). Honor implies obedience toward their parents and to God by putting God's moral commands into practice. The expectation is that this begins at a young age and increases steadily as they grow older. This commandment comes with a promise—a reward for bringing honor to one's parents. Also implied here and stated elsewhere is that failure to honor parents can result in serious consequences. This actually occurred many centuries later when all twelve tribes of Israel were exiled from their land. Both parents and their children failed to follow God's instructions. Behaviors have consequences.

While parents can and do make mistakes, children do as well, even with the best of parents. There are several passages that illustrate this.

> Children, obey our parents in everything, for this is pleases the Lord. (Colossians 3:20)

> Hear, O sons, a father's instruction, and be attentive, that you may gain insight. (Proverbs 4:1)

> Children, obey your parents in the Lord, for this is right. (Ephesians 6:1)

Children sometimes rebel against their parents and, in so doing, dishonor both them and God. The story of the prodigal son in Luke 15:11–32 is an illustration of what that may look like. The son disrespected and rebelled against his father and left home. This story has been replayed countless times around the world. Just as parents have the responsibility of teaching and disciplining their children, children have the responsibility of obeying and honoring their parents. In the earlier reference to Eli the priest, his two sons knew that their actions were wrong, and they were held accountable by God.

Our shortcomings as parents or children, however, need not be the end of the story. All parents and children make mistakes. God understands this completely and extends His mercy (not getting what we deserve) and grace (getting what we don't deserve) to all who repent, even after our children have become adults and turn to Him. As the psalmist David wrote, "God is gracious and compassionate, abounding in love" (Psalm 103:8). God's love for people is so great that He will forgive past sins, even the most serious ones. First John 1:9 says, "If we confess our sins, he is faithful and just to forgive us our sins and to cleanse us from all unrighteousness." The key is for anyone to admit their error and repent. He wants to restore us to fellowship with Him and welcomes all to him with open arms. Isn't that amazing? God's forgiveness is greater than any mistake we ever made. The story about the prodigal son did not end tragically. Rather, the son repented, and the father welcomed him back and restored him to full fellowship. This is a picture of what God, our Father, is willing to do for all who repent.

Parenting and raising children is serous and challenging work. While others may help reinforce their instruction, such as churches, schools, family, and neighbors, parents are primarily responsible for the moral training of their children. Children without such teaching and correction miss out and can easily be led astray as they become adults (or sooner). This need not be so.

6

LIVING IN VICTORY

But thanks be to God, who gives us the victory
through our Lord Jesus Christ.
—1 Corinthians 15:57

We often think of victory in terms of competition or contests where one individual or team is victorious. But there is a victory that surpasses all others; it is the victory we have over anything we encounter in this world that may control or defeat us. As stated in the verse above, we can achieve victory through Jesus Christ. We are able to have victory over addictions, anger, pride, interpersonal conflict, worry, sinful desires of every kind, and even death. If we put our faith and trust in Jesus, He will help us live a life of victory because He Himself is victorious over all. He has all authority over heaven and earth and is greater than any difficulty we may face. As a result, we can live life of victory that is filled with peace and joy.

In Revelation 17:14, we find these words: "They will make war on the Lamb, and the Lamb will conquer them, for he is Lord of lords and King of kings, and those with him are called and chosen and faithful." The Lamb refers to Jesus Christ, and He is the Lord of lords and the King of kings. In other words, He is ruler over all leaders on earth. In fact, He is the ruler over all things in this universe. He has overcome the forces of evil (Satan) through His victory over death on the cross and now reigns supreme over the heavens and the earth. Similarly, Matthew 28:18

states, "And Jesus came and said to them, "All authority in heaven and on earth has been given to me." Jesus is all-powerful; nothing is too hard for Him. The wonderful news is that Jesus's victory is something we can all share in. He overcame rejection, sorrow, sickness, and even death for our benefit. And He desires that His followers also live in victory. Though we may experience difficult circumstances and experience life's valleys, we need not remain there. Because He overcame and now lives, we too can overcome and live.

MASTERING MONEY

People treasure many things in this world, such as status, sports, power, friendships, and possessions, to mention a few. For many, money is the most treasured of all. They not only treasure it but allow it to dominate their lives. The Bible has much to teach about money and contains specific warnings about the love of money. Why is it so bad to treasure money? After all, who wants to be poor? Is it not possible to love money, things, and people equally? Let's explore what the Bible has to say about this.

The Bible explains that when we put money first, it leads us down the wrong path. In 1 Timothy 6:10, the apostle Paul said, "For the love of money is a root of all kinds of evil. Some people who are eager for money, have wandered from the faith and pierced themselves with many griefs" (NIV). Paul puts it plainly; all kinds of evil and grief result from putting money above all else. Paul did not say that money itself is the root of evil. It is of course possible to possess large amounts of money and manage it wisely. Rather, it is the love of money, being so focused on one's personal wealth that it becomes more important than anything else.

There are many reasons why this is so. First, money can dominate our thoughts and actions to the point that we no longer have a balanced and clear thought process. It can cause us to say or do things that are unwise and even dangerous. Those who love money rarely, if ever, have enough money. This drives the need to earn more and more, even though they are already very wealthy. When our focus is on money, it is not on those things that God values, and that's a problem.

Second, it is because money competes with God for our attention. In the first of the Ten Commandments, God made it clear that He comes first. "There must be no other God's before me" (Exodus 20:1). Anything that comes before God means that it interferes with our relationship with God, or worse, it takes the place of God. God says do not do this! He desires to be first in our lives. When we push God aside, we miss out on many things, such as blessings, wisdom, and peace. We lose touch with the very one (Jesus) who is most able to help us through life. And when that happens, we are given over to our own desires, and this then leads to all kinds of evil that Paul mentioned. Jesus spoke directly about this in Matthew 6:24 where He said, "No one can serve two masters, for either he will hate the one and love the other, or he will be devoted to the one and despise the other. You cannot serve God and money." Jesus did not say that it is difficult; He said you cannot!

Third, the love money comes with the risks of selfishness, greed, and unjust gain. Consider the following warnings:

> Such are the ways of everyone who is greedy for unjust gain; it takes away the life of its possessors. (Proverbs 1:19)

> Whoever is greedy for unjust gain troubles his own household, but he who hates bribes will live. (Proverbs 15:27)

> A stingy man hastens after wealth and does not know that poverty will come upon him. (Proverbs 28:22)

Greed can creep into person's life and eventually gain control over their thoughts and actions. This can lead to stealing, deceit, mistreatment of others, and even worse actions. God understands our nature completely and our strong tendencies toward selfishness and greed. This is why He warned us so many times. He also knows that if our focus is on Him rather than money, we will avoid many problems.

The fourth reason we are warned about loving money is because money cannot satisfy; it cannot bring lasting joy and happiness. God desires that we live productive and joy-filled lives and understands the deceitfulness of money and how it can cause heartaches and sorrow—just the opposite of what we think. The following passages help us see this:

> He who loves money will not be satisfied with money, nor he who loves wealth with his income; this also is vanity. (Ecclesiastes 5:10)

> Do not toil to acquire wealth; be discerning enough to desist. When your eyes light on it, it is gone, for suddenly it sprouts wings, flying like an eagle toward heaven. (Proverbs 23:4–5)

> Come now, you rich, weep and howl for the miseries that are coming upon you. Your riches have rotted and your garments are moth-eaten. Your gold and silver have corroded, and their corrosion will be evidence against you and will eat your flesh like fire. You have laid up treasure in the last days. Behold, the wages of the laborers who mowed your fields, which you kept back by fraud, are crying out against you, and the cries of the harvesters have reached the ears of the Lord of hosts. You have lived on the earth in luxury and in self-indulgence. You have fattened your hearts in a day of slaughter. (James 5:1–6)

King Solomon, who attained great wealth, eventually realized that pursuing riches is meaningless; it does not satisfy except perhaps temporarily. Mark 8:36 does a wonderful job of putting money in perspective: "For what does it profit a man to gain the whole world and forfeit his soul?" If we can become the wealthiest person on earth but miss out on eternal life (heaven), all wealth is for naught.

The last reason is because those who have money can become prideful and come to the conclusion that they do not need God; they are self-sufficient and have all they ever need in this world. They say, "We have earned everything without God's help." They believe their wealth was achieved through their own abilities and hard work and that they are in control of their own destiny. How sad and how foolish! They are so misguided that they cannot see that it was God who gifted them with the knowledge and skills to earn money. And it was God who gave them the health, intellect, skills, and circumstances that enabled them to accumulate wealth. Jesus told a story in Luke 12:16–21 that helps us to see this more clearly. Beginning in verse 18, we read, "The rich person was very proud of his accomplishments and decided to build bigger barns to hold all of his crops. Then he said, 'This is what I'll do. I will tear down my barns and build bigger ones, and there I will store my surplus grain. And I'll say to myself, "You have plenty of grain laid up for many years. Take life easy; eat, drink and be merry."' But God said to him, 'You fool! This very night your life will be demanded from you. Then who will get what you have prepared for yourself?' This is how it will be with whoever stores up things for themselves but is not rich toward God." The Bible teaches again and again that God is Sovereign over all; everything on this earth (and universe for that matter) belongs to Him, and He is master over everyone, both rich and poor. It is God who enables us with the ability to earn money. Everything we have comes from God. He is the great provider. God admonished the Israelites in this regard in Deuteronomy 8:13–14 before they entered the land of Canaan: "And when your herds and your flocks multiply, and your silver and gold multiply, and all that you have multiplies, Then your heart will become proud and you will forget the LORD your God who brought you out from the land of Egypt." In verse 17, God continues, "Otherwise, you may say in your heart, 'My power and the strength of my hand made me this wealth.' But you shall remember the LORD your God, for it is He who is giving you power to make wealth." It is God and God alone who provides us with the gifts and abilities to work and earn money. Even our health is a gift from God; He provides with the physical and mental capability of performing work. It is our responsibility to use what He has given us to bring honor and glory to Him. Proverbs 3:9 reinforces this principle: "Honor the LORD with your wealth, with the first fruits of all your crops." A key issue here is pride. It is easy to become proud of our accomplishments. But God opposes all those who are proud. Why? It is because pride interferes with our relationship with Him. It puts us at the center and not God. Pride is a terrible thing.

Mastering Money God's Way

How then should we become the master of our money instead of it mastering us? How should we gain a proper perspective on wealth, regardless of how little or how much we have? The Bible provides excellent wisdom to guide us. First and foremost, the Bible teaches that we must put God first. Consider Matthew 6:33 where it says, "But seek first the kingdom of God and his righteousness, and all these things will be added to you." And in Matthew 6:19–21, it says, "Do not lay up for yourselves treasures on earth, where moth and rust destroy and where thieves break in and steal, but lay up for yourselves treasures in heaven, where neither moth nor rust destroys and where thieves do not break in and steal. For where your treasure is, there your heart will be also." This means giving of your tithes and offerings to God (through the church), loving and serving others, helping and caring for those in need, and sharing the good news of the Gospel. Essentially, it means obeying all that Jesus commanded us to do. In 1 Timothy 6:17–19, Paul explained this very well: "As for the rich in this present age, charge them not to be haughty, nor to set their hopes on the uncertainty of riches, but on God, who richly provides us with everything to enjoy. They are to do good, to be rich in good works, to be generous and ready to share, thus storing up treasure for themselves as a good foundation."

Second, the Bible advises us to be content with whatever wealth God has blessed us with. Consider the following scripture passages:

> Behold, what I have seen to be good and fitting is to eat and drink and find enjoyment in all the toil with which one toils under the sun the few days of his life that God has given him, for this is his lot. Everyone also to whom God has given wealth and possessions and power to enjoy them, and to accept his lot and rejoice in his toil—this is the gift of God. For he will not much remember the days of his life because God keeps him occupied with joy in his heart. (Ecclesiastes 5:18–20)

Not that I am speaking of being in need, for I have learned in whatever situation I am to be content. I know how to be brought low, and I know how to abound. In any and every circumstance, I have learned the secret of facing plenty and hunger, abundance and need. I can do all things through him who strengthens me. (Philippians 4:11–13)

Keep your life free from love of money, and be content with what you have, for he has said, "I will never leave you nor forsake you." (Hebrews 13:5)

This does not mean that we sit back and let life happen or don't continue working hard. Rather, we are to be grateful for whatever we have at any time. We must not become envious of what others might have; that is not our concern. Our task is to do the absolute best with what God has given us. Otherwise, we risk the love of money and seeking more and more possessions. God is deeply opposed to this. God knows our needs and will provide for us. It is a matter of trust. The apostle Paul expressed this clearly in 1 Timothy 6:17 where he wrote, "As for the rich in this present age, charge them not to be haughty, nor to set their hopes on the uncertainty of riches, but on God, who richly provides us with everything to enjoy."

Lastly, in order to truly master money, it is important to practice giving willingly and generously (see the section on generosity). Giving away our money accomplishes three things. It helps those in need and those in ministry. Second, it is an act of worship that is honoring to God, as referred to earlier in Proverbs 3:9. When we give, we are trusting God that He will provide all our needs, and this is honoring to God. Third, we master our money by demonstrating that it does not have control over us. In Luke 12:33–34, Jesus said, "Sell your possessions, and give to the needy. Provide yourselves with moneybags that do not grow old, with a treasure in the heavens that does not fail, where no thief approaches and no moth destroys. For where your treasure is, there will your heart be also." By giving with a willing heart, we demonstrate that we can let go of material possessions—they have no grip on us. When we give, we are storing up treasures in heaven, which are vastly more valuable than treasures on earth. There is some excellent advice found in 1 John 2:15–17, where we read, "Do not love the world or the things in the world. If anyone loves the world, the love of the Father is not in him. For all that is in the world—the desires of the flesh and the desires of the eyes and pride in possessions—is not from the Father but is from the world. And the world is passing away along with its desires, but whoever does the will of God abides forever."

Someday we all must leave our earthly possessions behind and face death. Who knows what will happen to our money? God does! After all, it all belongs to Him.

OVERCOMING ANGER

Some things can cause us to become irritated and even deeply upset, which can lead to the strong emotion of displeasure called anger. Words and/or actions of others can provoke anger when things don't go our way. These can cause great displeasure and even infuriate us. Although anger is part of our human nature, it need not consume us. With God's help, we can overcome anger.

As one might expect, the Bible has important things to teach us about anger. It treats anger as a serious matter and especially warns us about letting our anger get out of control. In Matthew 5:21–22, Jesus said, "You have heard that our ancestors were told, 'You must not murder. If you commit murder, you are subject to judgment.' But I say, if you are even angry with someone, you are subject to judgment! If you call someone an idiot, you are in danger of being brought before the court. And if you curse someone, you are in danger of the fires of hell" (NLT). The Bible teaches that there are a number of issues with anger, which are outlined below.

Anger Can Lead to Sin

One of the key issues with anger is that it can lead to words or actions that have evil intent; anger can become sinful—wrong in God's eyes. Anger can result in yelling and shouting things we really don't mean, uncontrolled outrage, hatred, aggression, and violence. Uncontrolled, it can cause great harm to others and to one's self—either emotional or physical. In Ephesians 4:26–27, we read, "Be angry, and yet do not sin; do not let the sun go down on your anger, and do not give the devil an opportunity." If we do become angry, it is important to resolve the matter quickly; don't allow anger to linger in your mind. This principle also is taught in other scripture passages. Consider the following (from the NLT):

> Do not nurse hatred in your heart for any of your relatives. Confront people directly so you will not be held guilty for their sin. (Leviticus 19:17)

> Stop being angry! Turn from your rage! Do not lose your temper—it only leads to harm. (Psalm 37:8)

> A man of wrath stirs up strife, and one given to anger causes much transgression. (Proverbs 29:22)

> When you follow the desires of your sinful nature, the results are very clear: sexual immorality, impurity, lustful pleasures, idolatry, sorcery, hostility, quarreling, jealousy, outbursts of anger, selfish ambition, dissension, division. (Galatians 5:19–20)

> Understand this, my dear brothers and sisters: You must all be quick to listen, slow to speak, and slow to get angry. Human anger does not produce the righteousness God desires. (James 1:19–20)

The advice from the Bible is clear; anger is something we can and must manage in our lives. Anger that lingers in our minds is anger that can control us, which is never good.

Anger Is Unwise

Consider the following verses (NASB):

> For anger slays the foolish man, And jealousy kills the simple. (Job 5:2)

> Do not be eager in your heart to be angry, for anger resides in the hearts of fools. (Ecclesiastes 7:9)

> A fool's anger is known at once, but a prudent man conceals dishonor. (Proverbs 12:16)

> A quick-tempered man acts foolishly, and a man of evil devices is hated. (Proverbs 14:17)

> He who is slow to anger has great understanding, But he who is quick-tempered exalts foolishness. (Proverbs 14:29)

> A fool's anger is known at once, but a wise man conceals dishonor. (Proverbs 29:11)

Notice that in each passage, anger is not only unwise but is treated as foolish. It is foolish because it rarely accomplishes anything but instead can cause harm to ourselves and to others. A lifestyle of anger can even have significant negative effects on physical and mental health.

Jesus Controlled His Anger

As we look at the life of Jesus, there are several things that caused Him to become angry, such as hypocrisy, rules that kept people from God, injustice, and selfishness. Though Jesus became angry, His responses were aimed at teaching and correcting. He dealt with each situation immediately and for the benefit of those who needed to change. There are things in this world that should move us to anger, such as injustice, violence, abuse, and starvation. It is not that we should never get angry; rather, it is a matter of what we do with that anger. When under control, anger can lead to positive things—words or actions that correct and improve. When tempered with love, kindness, and respect, anger can lead to positive change. Even though we may be angry at something or someone, the Bible teaches that this is no excuse to forget all the things that Jesus taught us about loving our neighbors as ourselves. The warnings in the Bible about anger are clear, but so are the solutions.

In Ephesians 4:31–32, Paul wrote, "Let all bitterness and wrath and anger and clamor and slander be put away from you, along with all malice. Be kind to one another, tender-hearted, forgiving each other, just as God in Christ also has forgiven you." We are to put things like anger and wrath behind us and strive toward a lifestyle of kindness and forgiveness. This is what a follower of Jesus does. They do these things because they help us become more Christlike, which is our goal. We do this because our role model, Jesus, did this and expects this from us as well. This theme is also found in the Old Testament. In Psalm 145:8, it says, "The Lord is gracious and merciful; slow to anger and great in lovingkindness." And in Psalm 30:4–5, we read, "Sing praise to the Lord, you His godly ones, and give thanks to His holy name. For His anger is but for a moment, his favor is for a lifetime; weeping may last for the night, but a shout of joy comes in the morning." We too must be slow to anger, and if anger should come, it lasts for but a moment. To be Christlike means to have the same attitude as Christ toward others. We must heed the advice from Paul in Colossians 3:8, "But now you also, put them all aside: anger, wrath, malice, slander, and abusive speech from your mouth."

How then can we control our anger? The book of Proverbs contains great wisdom for many subjects, and anger is no exception. Consider the wise advice provided in these passages:

A hot-tempered man stirs up strife, But the slow to anger calms a dispute. (Proverbs 15:18)

A man's discretion makes him slow to anger, and it is his glory to overlook a transgression. (Proverbs 19:11)

He who is slow to anger is better than the mighty, and he who rules his spirit, than he who captures a city. (Proverbs 16:32)

The phrase *slow to anger* is attributed to God in numerous Old Testament passages, so it is not surprising that it is found in wisdom literature. These passages teach us the importance of self-control. Being slow to anger means to be patient understanding with others, making sure we listen, are quick to forgive, and seek God's wisdom in the matter. Followers of Jesus are not easily offended and are quick to extend grace to others. They think before they allow their emotions to control their words and deeds. This was made clear by Paul in 1 Corinthians 13:4–5, "Love is patient, love is kind. It does not envy, it does not boast, it is not proud. It is not rude, it is not self-seeking, it is not easily angered, it keeps no record of wrongs" (NIV). This is a wonderful teaching—love for others is able to overcome feelings of anger.

A second way we can learn to prevent anger is to avoid people who are quick to anger. Instead, it is advisable to associate with people who model self-control. In Proverbs 22:24–25, it says, "Do not associate with a man given to anger; or go with a hot-tempered man, or you will learn his ways and find a snare for yourself." We are greatly influenced by those around us. Choose your friends wisely.

A third way to overcome anger is to resolve to never get revenge for a wrong. In Romans 12:19, Paul wrote, "Never take your own revenge, beloved, but leave room for the wrath of God, for it is written, 'Vengeance is Mine, I will repay,' says the Lord." Never means never. And in Psalm 7:11, we read, "God is a righteous judge, And a God who has indignation every day." It is not our place to judge and seek revenge on others. This is God's business.

A fourth way to avoid anger is to choose our words carefully. This seems to be difficult for most of us. Nevertheless, it is most wise. Proverbs 15:1 says, "A gentle answer turns away wrath, but a harsh word stirs up anger." During my lifetime, I have observed both aspects of this Proverb numerous times and can attest to its accuracy. Gentle answers are always the wise choice. This is reinforced in Proverbs 17:27, where it says, "He who restrains his words has knowledge, and he who has a cool spirit is a man of understanding." With the help of the Holy Spirit, we can learn to control our words and thus show our commitment to Jesus's teachings.

Lastly, there is excellent advice to parents. In Ephesians 6:4, Paul wrote, "Fathers, do not provoke your children to anger, but bring them up in the discipline and instruction of the Lord." How might we provoke children in anger? Many mistakes that parents make can contribute to anger. Showing favoritism, not listening, mistreatment, public embarrassment, inconsistency, hypocrisy, and punishment without love are a few examples of things that can lead to resentment and anger in children, especially teenagers. No parent is perfect, but those who strive to avoid these and instead work toward teaching and modeling avoid provoking anger.

OVERCOMING GRIEF

Closely related to pain and suffering is the topic of grief, and it may even be considered a form of pain and suffering. This is a natural but unwelcomed part of life. At some point, we all experience grief, and for some, many times. Often, grief is caused by some type of loss, such as death, but can arrive in many ways; loss of resources, injuries, work situations, family, friends, and neighbors can all be sources of grief. It can consume us and may linger for years. It can even cause physical as well as emotional pain. We are usually unprepared for its arrival, and it has no scheduled time of departure.

Many Bible characters experienced grief, beginning with Adam and Eve after the murder of their son Abel by another son Cain. That must have been devastating for them. Other examples include Samson's parents, stemming from his behavior, David from the loss of his sons, Jeremiah from rejection and mistreatment, and Job from the loss of health, children, servants, and all his possessions. The book of Job reveals a story of overwhelming grief. Job's grief was so great that it left his friends speechless. Job 2:13 says, "And they sat with him on the ground seven days and seven nights, and no one spoke a word to him, for they saw that his grief was very great." In Genesis 23:2, the patriarch Abraham grieved following the death of his wife, Sarah; "And Sarah died at Kiriath-arba (that is, Hebron) in the land of Canaan, and Abraham went in to mourn for Sarah and to weep for her." And King David expressed grief over a sin he committed; "For my life is spent with sorrow, and my years with sighing; my strength fails because of my iniquity, and my bones waste away" (Psalm 31:10). In each of these cases, grief came in varying degrees and forms.

During His ministry on earth, Jesus experienced unimaginable grief. He suffered greatly at the hands of men by their rejection, hurtful words, and actions. Many centuries earlier, Isaiah 53:3 foretold Jesus's suffering: "He is despised and rejected of men; a man of sorrows, and acquainted with grief: and we hid as it were our faces from him; he was despised, and we esteemed him not." Jesus was literally despised by the religious leaders who did not acknowledge Him as the promised Messiah and deeply resented Jesus's claim that He was. During His trial, He was abandoned by His disciples, falsely accused, mocked, beaten, and then put to death in a most painful way, on a cross. Though innocent of any wrongdoing, He bore the sins of the entire world upon His shoulders. Jesus understood grief and the grieving process. He wept in response to the death of His friend Lazarus (John 11:35). But Jesus's grief is good news for us. He can relate to our situations completely; He understands our emotions and pain. In Psalm 34:18, we read, "The Lord is close to the brokenhearted and saves those who are crushed in spirit." And similarly, in Psalm 147:3, we read, "He heals the brokenhearted and binds up their wounds." God is compassionate and gracious (103:8) and wants to help us overcome our grief. The Bible tells us that there are several ways this occurs.

Through scripture! God helps us through scripture passages. God's Word brings comfort and hope to all who grieve. Consider the passage in 2 Corinthians 1:3–4, "Blessed be the God and Father of our Lord Jesus Christ, the Father of mercies and God of all comfort, who comforts us in all our affliction, so that we may be able to comfort those who are in any affliction, with the comfort with which we ourselves are comforted by God." And in Psalm 46:1–2, we read, "God is our refuge and strength, a very present help in trouble. Therefore we will not fear, though the earth should change and though the mountains slip into the heart of the sea."

Through people! Friends, family, neighbors, and even strangers can be of great help for those who are grieving. They can listen, provide comfort, encourage, and more. The Bible instructs us to come alongside and comfort those who are grieving. Romans 12:5 says, "Rejoice with those who rejoice, mourn with those who mourn" (NIV). And in Proverbs 17:17, we read, "A friend loves at all times, and a brother is born for adversity." A friend who is physically present (or through other means of communication) can help someone through even the most difficult of circumstances.

Through Jesus! Jesus's love is so vast that He literally would do anything for us. In fact, He did; He gave His life for us. In John 12:15 is written one of the most profound truths in the Bible; we can claim Jesus as our friend. Jesus said, "I no longer have called you servants, because a servant does not know his master's business. Instead I have called you friend, for everything that I have learned from the Father I have made known to you." It is of great comfort to know that you have a forever friend who loves you, cares deeply for you, and is there each day—for you. One never needs to be alone in their grief. Just ask, and Jesus will be there for you.

Jesus helps us through the Holy Spirit. While still on earth, Jesus promised that the Holy Spirit would be available abundantly for all who believe and put their trust in Him. The Holy Spirit is our personal comforter and counselor and available all day every day. John 14:16 says, "And I will ask the Father, and he shall give you another Helper, to be with you forever." The Holy Spirit is one's personal helper; He comforts, guides, teaches, and much more. The apostle Paul wrote in Romans 8:26–27, "Likewise the Spirit helps in our weaknesses. For we do not know what we should pray for as we ought, but the Spirit himself intercedes for us with groanings too deep for words. And He who searches the hearts knows what is the mind of the Spirit, because the Spirit intercedes for the saints according to the will of God." In our darkest times, the Holy Spirit is present to remind us of scripture passages that provide comfort, guide friends to help is, speak words of encouragement to us either directly or through others, and even pray for us. With God, we are never alone. We only need to seek Him and ask for help. James 4:8 says, "Draw near to God and He will draw near to you." God provides the confidence and hope that we will overcome our grief and sorrow.

Through restoration! Grief is a process, and usually there is a time of healing recovery. God promises that He will restore us; He wants us to overcome our grief and continue to live a fulfilled life. In Psalm 23:3, David writes, "He restores my soul." God sees us through to the other side of the darkest valley. We have the hope and assurance that one day our grief and sorrow will be behind us. After Job experienced overwhelming disaster in his life, he was restored. In Job 42:10, it says, "The LORD made him prosperous again and gave him twice as much as he had before." Notice that it was God's hand at work, not through the efforts of Job. God has plans for each of us—to overcome grief and live in victory. Consider Jeremiah 29:11, "'For I know the plans I have for you,' declares the LORD, 'plans to prosper you and not to harm you, plans to give you hope and a future'"(NIV). God is a God of hope. While grief is real, it is also temporary.

In the midst of our grief, we seldom can understand the reasons for it. Sometimes we resort to blaming ourselves, blaming others, or even God. But the Bible assures us that God sees the bigger picture, how this can help us grow spiritually and how we can grow closer to Him. Romans 8:28 says, "And we know that for those who love God, all things work together for good for those who are called according to His purpose." God sees our grief and knows our pain. But He also sees the path to recovery, which may be hidden from us. There may be benefits to our grief not only to ourselves but to those around us. Our role is to ask for His help and trust that He will provide a way.

The Bible reminds us again and again that earth is our temporary home and we should not become too attached to it or be surprised when we grieve. Jesus promised that in this world you will have trouble (John 16:33). And He reminded us that He has overcome the world and that there is something better awaiting all those who put their faith in Him. Jesus gave this promise in Revelation 21:4, "He will wipe away every tear from their eyes, and death shall be no more, neither shall there be mourning, nor crying, nor pain anymore, for the former things have passed away." Heaven is our future home, where there is eternal rejoicing; no more grief or sorry will be there. The words of Psalm 91:1–2 are a reminder to everyone that we are never alone in our grief; "He who stands in the shelter of the Most High will rest in the shadow of the almighty. I will say of the Lord, "He is my refuge and my fortress, my God in whom I trust" (NIV). Grief is real, but so are God's promises that He cares and will help us overcome it.

OVERCOMING PAIN AND SUFFERING

Pain and suffering may be physical or emotional and occur in every imaginable way and in every society. From the beginning of the very first book of the Bible, we find examples of individuals who experienced pain and suffering, and there is much to gain by examining their experiences. While explaining the reasons for pain and suffering are beyond the scope of this section, we will see how several Bible characters coped with their circumstances.

One Bible character who stands out relative to suffering is described in the book of Job.

Job was a wealthy man who lost everything, including his health. And though he lived thousands of years ago, he is someone with whom we can relate to today. Job was a righteous man who feared God. Seemingly everything was going well in his life—family, business, possessions, servants, and recognition. But then disaster struck; he lost his livestock, servants, and all his children. Within a short time, it was all gone, and he was overwhelmed with sorrow. If that were not enough, he was afflicted with painful sores over his body. After all this great tragedy, Job's suffering was multiplied in the form of accusation by his three friends. They falsely accused him of being sinful and deserving this punishment. Surely there was some grievous sin that Job was hiding. The text, however, assures us that there was not. God had allowed Satan to attack Job. Job arguably suffered as much as any person who has ever lived (except Jesus). He could not understand why this had happened to him and even questioned

God's motives. In all this trouble, though, he remained faithful to God and realized that there were many things he did not understand. God restored Job, including possessions and children. Through this experience, Job learned that his relationship with God was more important than anything else—family, possessions, health included. Suffering brings one in a closer, deeper relationship with God. He also learned that God is infinitely wise and has reasons for actions that are beyond our understanding. Job experienced a change within himself; elements of pride and self-righteousness were purged. Job's faith grew stronger, as did his trust in God.

One question that could be asked of Job is whether anything can be learned or gained from his suffering. Is pain and suffering entirely negative, or is there something positive to be gained? The answer is clearly yes. What Job (and many others) learned is this: whatever it takes to bring us closer to God is worth it. You see, the Bible teaches that our relationship with God must be primary in our life. It must surpass all earthly possessions and relationships. King Solomon had everything that life could offer, but in the end, he found it all meaningless. In Ecclesiastes 1:14, Solomon admitted, "I observed everything going on under the sun, and really, it is all meaningless—like chasing the wind" (NLT). But later, in Ecclesiastes 12:13, Solomon reflected on all his experiences and put it this way: "Now all has been heard; here is the conclusion of the matter: fear God and keep his commandments, for this is the duty of all mankind." Meaning and purpose in life in not found in possessions; rather, they are found in a deep, trusting relationship with God. God may or may not choose to allow suffering to occur in our lives. Either way, we are to trust His wisdom. We have a choice as to how we respond to pain and suffering. God sees our lives as temporary. Earth is not our final home; heaven is. God wants to develop our character to the fullest extent for His purposes and His glory. In Romans 5:3–5, Paul states, "More than that, we rejoice in our sufferings, knowing that suffering produces endurance, and endurance produces character, and character produces hope, and hope does not put us to shame, because God's love has been poured into our hearts through the Holy Spirit who has been given to us." And later in Romans 8:18, Paul further states, "For I consider that the sufferings of this present time are not worth comparing with the glory that is to be revealed to us." There is something far greater that awaits those who put their hope and trust in Jesus Christ. The reward is eternity in heaven. It is worth anything that we might encounter here on earth. Many other passages like these encourage us to remain faithful through periods of suffering, even deep, painful suffering.

How then should we respond to suffering? Here are some things that we can do:

- Spend time in prayer asking God for strength and guidance.
- Look for the greater good. *What is God teaching me?*
- Recognize that God treasures our love for Him.
- Believe in the absolute sovereignty of God.
- Believe that God does everything right and good. (Romans 8:28: "And we know that for those who love God all things work together for good, for those who are called according to his purpose.")
- Repent of times when you have questioned God or blamed God.
- If you are suffering for your faith in Jesus, consider James 1:2–4: "Count it all joy, my brothers, when you meet trials of various kinds, for you know that the testing of your faith produces steadfastness. And let steadfastness have its full effect, that you may be perfect and complete, lacking in nothing."

Consider these words of wisdom from Hebrews 11:32–40:

And what more shall I say? I do not have time to tell about Gideon, Barak, Samson and Jephthah, about David and Samuel and the prophets, who through faith conquered kingdoms, administered justice, and gained what was promised; who shut the mouths of lions, quenched the fury of the flames, and escaped the edge of the sword; whose weakness was turned to strength; and who became powerful in battle and routed foreign armies. Women received back their dead, raised to life again. There were others who were tortured, refusing to be released so that they might gain an even better resurrection. Some faced jeers and flogging, and even chains and imprisonment. They were put to death by stoning; they were sawed in two; they were killed by the sword. They went about in sheepskins and goatskins, destitute, persecuted and mistreated—the world was not worthy of them. They wandered in deserts and mountains, living in caves and in holes in the ground. These were all commended for their faith, yet none of them received what had been promised, since God had planned something better for us so that only together with us would they be made perfect.

These heroes of the faith endured great pain and suffering, but there was something better that awaited them—eternal life. And were they to testify before us today they would say, "It was well worth it."

We can also learn much about pain and suffering from the apostle Paul. After becoming a follower of Jesus, Paul became a committed evangelist who planted churches throughout the Middle East, Asia Minor, and southern Europe. During his missionary travels, he met stiff resistance in many places. Paul describes his challenges this way in 2 Corinthians 11:24–27: "Five times I received from the Jews thirty-nine lashes. Three times I was beaten with rods, once I was stoned, three times I was shipwrecked, a night and a day I have spent in the deep. I have been on frequent journeys, in dangers from rivers, dangers from robbers, dangers from my countrymen, dangers from the Gentiles, dangers in the city, dangers in the wilderness, dangers on the sea, dangers among false brethren; I have been in labor and hardship, through many sleepless nights, in hunger and thirst, often without food, in cold and exposure." Not many of us experience these kinds of thing. Paul's response to all of these could have been bitterness, anger, disillusionment, or even hatred for God. But it wasn't. Rather, Paul said it was all worth it. In 2 Corinthians 12:10, Paul wrote, "For the sake of Christ, then, I am content with weaknesses, insults, hardships, persecutions, and calamities. For when I am weak, then I am strong." Paul understood that there is something better that awaits us. He faced all these things willingly and with joy.

Another Bible character who experienced pain and suffering was the prophet Jeremiah. He experienced the following: the people rejected his message, he was beaten and put in stocks, was given a death sentence, had a scroll that he had carefully written burned, was thrown into a pit and left to die, and was despised and called a liar (even though he told the truth). Jeremiah stood alone as the voice of God to warn his people of severe punishment unless they repented. He faced great pain and suffering not because he deserved it or by happenstance but out of obedience and love for God. Jeremiah obeyed God even though it meant suffering. Why? The same reason all the other prophets who experienced pain and suffering did, because they counted the cost of being God's servant. To them, it was worth it.

Jesus's suffering, as described in the four Gospels (Matthew, Mark, Luke, and John), was extreme. He not only experienced great physical suffering but also mental anguish. Though he was completely innocent, He was verbally and physically abused and put to death in one of the cruelest ways known to mankind—crucifixion. And yet Jesus faced all this willingly because He knew the greater purpose in His life and death. And Jesus can personally relate to any pain and suffering that we may experience and sympathizes with us. He showed us how to face pain and suffering but also how to overcome it. There is much comfort for us in knowing that the object of our faith, Jesus, experienced great suffering. He did this for us. He understands completely what it means to suffer greatly, even to death. He can sympathize with our pain and sorrow completely. The best thing is that He is not only our Savior but also our friend. No matter what, where, or when, Jesus is our forever friend who will always listen and cares more deeply for us than we can ever imagine.

The Bible clearly indicates that we should not expect a life of ease. Life comes complete with pain and suffering in every imaginable form. But it also teaches that our attitude toward it matters. Whether physical or emotional suffering, we must learn to grow from our darkest valleys, and in doing so, become mature in our faith. And we must remember that pain and suffering are only temporary. One day, suffering will cease to exist, as we are told in Revelation 21:4: "He will wipe away every tear from their eyes, and death shall be no more, neither shall there be mourning, nor crying, nor pain anymore, for the former things have passed away." I trust that you are as anxious for that day to come as I am.

OVERCOMING TEMPTATION

To be tempted means to be lured or enticed to do or say something. We are attracted or drawn because we desire it. In the Bible, temptation refers to something that entices us toward doing something wrong; it conflicts with God's moral law. We are tempted to do many things, such as lying, cheating, stealing, lusting, adultery, gluttony, boasting, coveting, being greedy, and slandering. Temptations can come at any time, in any place, and in any form, and they come often. The Bible makes the distinction between being tempted to do something wrong and actually doing the wrong. Temptation by itself is not wrong or sinful; it is when we give in that it becomes sin.

Sometimes the desire to do something wrong is strong, so much so that resisting seems difficult, if not impossible. But there is good news. God understands our human nature and knows that we are weak and vulnerable, and He provided the necessary defense mechanisms. In 1 Corinthians 10:13, Paul wrote, "No temptation has overtaken you that is not common to man. God is faithful, and he will not let you be tempted beyond your ability, but with the temptation he will also provide the way of escape, that you may be able to endure it." This is a promise! Temptations need not overtake us because God is faithful, understands our ability to withstand them, and provides protection. Notice that God also provides a way out, an exit from the temptation. The temptation may not go away, but a way is provided so that we can resist and overcome them.

Let's go just a little deeper with this because it is of utmost importance. In James 1:14–15, we find this statement: "But each person is tempted when he is lured and enticed by his own desire. Then desire when it has conceived gives birth to sin, and sin when it is fully grown brings forth death." We are enticed by our own desire, meaning that it comes from within us. Desire here can also mean coveting—having a deep yearning for something. Such yearnings or desires can consume us to the point that we will do almost anything to have it, even if it means doing evil. Where does this yearning or desire come from? James says that it comes from within us—from our heart. Thinking about something and coveting or desiring it gives birth to sin, which can cause great harm to us—even destroy us. James says that this leads to death, which here refers not to physical death but spiritual death, which is far more serious.

Temptations come from our own desires and from Satan, who makes sin look attractive and desirable to us. It is Satan's wish to lead all astray—away from God and toward doing wrong, and he will do anything possible to accomplish this. Satan is our enemy who lies to us, tries to deceive us, and tempts us. We must be alert to his tactics. Temptation, then, is not just some harmless thing that we can ignore; it must be dealt with and overcome. Below are six strategies that can help us overcome temptations.

Flee from temptation. When confronted with temptation, the best approach may be to simply leave the scene. There is a story about a young man, Joseph, (Genesis 39) who was sold into slavery in Egypt and later became a servant in a prominent Egyptian official. One day, the wife of the official attempted to seduce Joseph, but instead of giving in, he chose to flee. He literally ran from trouble; there was no hesitation. What helped Joseph and can help you is to make up your mind to flee even before temptation occurs.

Change the thought. Thoughts can be harmful to us, as we saw in the James passage above. In Mark 7:21–22, Jesus said, "For from within, out of the heart of man, come evil thoughts, sexual immorality, theft, murder, adultery, coveting, wickedness, deceit, sensuality, envy, slander, pride, foolishness." There is a potent verse from Proverbs that reminds us of the importance of our thoughts. In verse 23:7, we read, "For as he thinks in his heart, so is he." (NLT) When we set our minds on things that we ought not do or say, we are more likely to act on those thoughts. Get rid of these. Replace evil thoughts with those that are pleasing to God. The apostle Paul provided some great advice for us in Philippians 4:8: "Finally, brothers, whatever is true, whatever is honorable, whatever is just, whatever is pure, whatever is lovely, whatever is commendable, if there is any excellence, if there is anything worthy of praise, think about these things." We have the ability (and responsibility) to choose the right things to think about.

Wear God's armor. There is every kind of evil in this world, and there is someone (Satan) who would like nothing better than to lead us astray. But we with God's help, we can take a stand against all things evil. In Ephesians 6:10–11, Paul advised us to be strong in the Lord and put on the armor of God. We have the following tools at our disposal:

- Belt of truth. This comes first because it is the foundation for everything else. Seek and know the truth about who we are and who we belong to—Jesus. Jesus is truth.
- Breastplate of righteousness. This protects our hearts from evil and comes through the acceptance of Jesus as our Savior.
- Shoes of the Gospel of peace. Have sure footing by being anchored in God's Word and being a person of peace, not conflict.
- Shield of faith. The shield (our faith in God) protects us against the attacks of Satan.
- Helmut of salvation. Salvation comes by grace through faith in Christ. When we accept Jesus as our Savior, He gives us the strength to fight evil of every kind.
- Sword of the Spirit. This is the word of God (The Bible), which enables us to go on the offensive in our battle against evil.

Avoid situations. Often, the best course of action is to simply avoid situations (or people who contribute to temptation). For example, attending events or activities in which wrongful things are taking place exposes us to needless temptation. Parents teach their children not to play with matches because they can be dangerous and the child (and/or someone else) may get hurt. There are countless things like matches we encounter throughout our lives that can and do cause harm. In other cases, when tempted, we can simply walk away (or even run).

Pray. In the prayer that Jesus taught, sometimes referred to as the Lord's Prayer, we find this phrase: "And lead us not into temptation, but deliver us from evil" (Matthew 6:13). Jesus invites us to ask for deliverance from evil. While God allows temptation in our lives, He will never personally tempt us. He will guide us away, from, and around temptation that may lead toward sin. Jesus will always help and loves it when we ask. We can pray for deliverance for specific temptations but also ask for protection each day. Many a temptation in my life has disappeared simply by keeping my focus on Jesus.

Memorize scripture. Finally, memorizing scripture is an effective way to resist temptation because God's Word is powerful. Jesus used scripture to resist Satan when tempted in the wilderness (Matthew chapter 4). Bible verses help us shift our focus from the temptation to God, and we draw on His strength during our times of weakness. God uses countless other ways to protect us. Take the time to select a verse or set of verses that you find helpful or inspiring and commit them to memory. Many excellent verses are found within this book. As situations arise, recite the verse(s) as often as necessary.

We do not need to fall victim to temptation because there is always a way out. We have control over what we see, read, hear, experience, and do because we have a friend at our side who is in control of all things in this world—Jesus. We can overcome.

OVERCOMING WORRY

People worry about many things, such as health, employment, money, family, safety, security, future events, crops, friendships, exams, and even the weather. Almost anything can cause one to worry. When someone worries about something, they think about or dwell on some challenge or problem. They go over it again and again in their mind, and sometimes it can dominate all other thoughts. Some individuals worry about one thing or another almost every day. A concern differs from worry in that a concern captures someone's attention, which they care about very much. A concern can trigger action, doing something about the issue, whereas worry is like an exercise wheel for animals that spins in place; it leads nowhere.

Worry is addressed in the Bible in a number of places, and in each case, it is viewed in negative terms. Worry is simply something we should not do. Several reasons are given why this is so.

In Proverbs 12:25, Solomon wrote, "Anxiety in a man's heart weighs him down, but a good word makes him glad." Being anxious about an issue can weigh us down to the point that it is debilitating. It can prevent us from functioning normally at home or at work and can lead to discouragement and fear. Issues can become overwhelming. Conversely, good words provide encouragement, dispelling fear and inspiring and instilling confidence; they help overcome worry. Also in Proverbs, we find these words in chapter 29:25: "The fear of man lays a snare, but whoever trusts in the LORD is safe." Solomon is saying that if we are afraid or anxious about what people may say or do, we miss out on the safety and security that comes with putting one's trust in God.

> So do not fear, for I am with you; do not be dismayed, for I am your God. I will strengthen you and help you; I will uphold you with my righteous right hand. (Isaiah 41:10 NIV)

> Peace I leave with you; my peace I give to you. Not as the world gives do I give to you. Let not your hearts be troubled, neither let them be afraid. (John 14:27 NIV).

> I have said these things to you, that in me you may have peace. In the world you will have trouble. But take heart; I have overcome the world. (John 16:33 NIV)

> So we can confidently say, The Lord is my helper; I will not fear; what can man do to me? (Hebrews 13:6)

In each of these passages, the message is consistent and clear: put your trust and hope in God and leave your cares to Him. This leaves us with the question of what do we do with our worries? In Psalm 55:22, it says, "Cast your burden on the LORD, and he will sustain you." And the apostle Peter advises us to cast all our anxieties on Him (1 Peter 5:6–7). How do we cast our burdens and worries on the Lord? There are three important things we can do. First, bring our concerns to God in prayer, as instructed in Philippians 4:6. As mentioned in the chapter on prayer, God invites us to bring everything to Him and assures us that He will listen to us. Second, develop a plan to address the concern. God will not only listen to our prayers, but He will help us determine the steps we should take (as needed). Third, the Bible advises us to seek the counsel of others. Seek those who understand the concern and are able to provide sound advice. God uses people to help us see through problems and enables them with wisdom. We may not be able to change things, but God certainly can, which brings peace in our hearts.

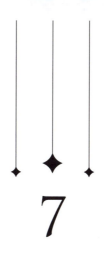

7

PERSONAL AND PROFESSIONAL SUCCESS

And may the Lord our God show us his approval
and make our efforts successful.
—Psalm 90:17 (NLT)

The Bible is an unlikely source for practical applications in the professional world, but it has an abundance of sound advice for us. The principle is that God wants to be involved in every aspect of our lives—at home, our leisure time, and also while working. Many men and women have learned this and have made Jesus the cornerstone of their professional success. Biblical thinking permeates their thought process, and they find great joy in serving God through activities such as leading, decision-making, and planning.

DECISION-MAKING

We make countless decisions during our lives. We begin at a very young age deciding which toy to play with or game to play. As we mature, many of our decisions take on increasing importance as we enter adulthood. Daily we make small choices—what time we rise or retire for the night, what to eat, what to wear, and the like. But we also make major decisions, such as career choice, friendships to pursue, who to marry, which house or car to buy, which hobbies to pursue, and how to manage our finances. We are free to make all kinds of decisions. The Bible contains wonderful advice on this topic. Although it does not prescribe a step-by-step guide to decision-making, it does provide general principles by which decisions are made.

Not all decisions we make are good ones, and most of us can recall ones that we regret. We are by no means alone and can find plenty of examples of people in the Bible who also made a poor decision. Adam and Eve chose to disobey God and ate fruit that was off-limits. Abraham chose to lie about his wife to a king so that he would be protected. King David decided to have one of his soldiers killed in battle and then tried to cover it up. King Rehoboam listened to unwise advisers, and it cost him his kingdom. Peter lied about his relationship with Jesus and regretted it soon after. We all have a sinful nature and can make poor choices at any time. Poor decisions, however, are avoidable—if we follow the Bible's guidance. The words found in Proverbs 3:5–6 (as mentioned elsewhere) contain excellent advice; "Trust in the Lord with all your heart and don't lean on your own understanding. In all your ways acknowledge Him and He will direct your paths." God will never steer you wrong.

I have learned that some decisions are easy because God opens or closes doors and makes the choice obvious. The reasons for this may not be understood at first (if at all), but we simply need to trust His wisdom. Other times, there was no clear choice, and it seemed that God was silent. In these cases, I found it necessary to spend more time in prayer and waiting for the answer, or simply making a decision and then asking for God's blessing and peace of mind. If you do not find peace with it, consider an alternative.

God has many ways that He communicates with us and guides our paths. He is always faithful and completely trustworthy. "For I know the plans I have for you, declares the LORD, plans for welfare and not for evil, to give you a future and a hope" (Jeremiah 29:11). Isn't it amazing that we have access to the best advice possible for every decision we might face? And this advice comes from someone who always has our best interest in mind. The Bible gives us this assurance. Below are several biblical guidelines for decision-making.

Be humble. Pride can interfere with our ability to think clearly about our options. We assume we understand everything or avoid asking for help because we don't want to admit any sign of weakness. But Proverbs 11:2 says, "When pride comes, then comes disgrace, but with the humble is wisdom." And similarly, Proverbs 15:33 provides this advice: "The fear of the LORD is instruction in wisdom, and humility comes before honor." The Bible indicates that asking for help is a sign of strength and wisdom.

Ask God. God is all-knowing (omniscient) and therefore always knows which choice is best for you. If you are ever in doubt, ask God. While He will never make our decisions for us, He invites us to ask His advice, and He is always delighted to help. To seek God's wisdom is to simply ask Him through prayer. James 1:5 says, "If any of you lacks wisdom, he should ask God, who gives generously to all without finding fault, and it will be given to him." First Chronicles 16:11 offers this advice: "Seek the Lord and his strength; seek his presence continually!" In Old Testament times, decisions were sometimes made by casting lots, which was often done using small stones. This was equivalent to throwing dice or drawing straws and was intended to yield unbiased decisions. The decision appeared to be by chance alone, but note what it says in Proverbs 16:33, "The lot is cast into the lap, but its every decision is from the Lord." The casting of lots was a way of choosing similar to drawing straws. But God was and is sovereign over all decisions, no matter how big or small. And if someone or something was chosen, it was with God's approval. And know this: God is never wrong. He will never give us bad advice.

Seek wise counsel from others. Proverbs 11:14 says, "Where there is no guidance, a nation falls, but in an abundance of counselors there is safety." In Proverbs 15:22, it says, "Without counsel plans fail, but with many advisers they succeed." And in Proverbs 18:1–24. we read. "Whoever isolates himself seeks his own desire; he breaks out against all sound judgment." From these passages, we see great wisdom. It is important, of course, to seek wise advisers who won't just tell us what we want to hear. Some individuals are gifted with wisdom, and God may use these people to help us with decisions. Some may view getting advice as a sign of weakness, but the Bible indicates that it is an indication of wisdom and maturity. There are two other proverbs that provide additional wisdom for decision-making. We must not only seek advice from others but also listen and apply the counsel. In Proverbs 12:15, it says, "The way of a fool is right in his own eyes, but a wise man listens to advice." Proverbs 19:20 provides similar wisdom: "Listen to advice and accept instruction, that you may gain wisdom in the future." One of the best advisers available is one's spouse. Husbands and wives often provide the best advice to each other. The lack of unity on a decision is a clear warning sign. It is not uncommon for God to use family, friends, and neighbors to deliver His guidance to us. Our challenge is to listen.

Evaluate whether the decision is within God's moral will. In other words, if a choice goes against any of God's laws (Ten Commandments in Exodus 20), this is clearly the wrong option. A decision may result in compromising one's values or lead to the oppression of others, which would be outside God's moral will. The Holy Spirit is available at all times for all situations to guide you toward the right or best choice. The key is to trust that God will help us to always make the best choice. This is stated clearly in Proverbs 3:5–6 mentioned above.

Evaluate your motives. In Proverbs 21:2, it says, "Every way of a man is right in his own eyes, but the LORD weighs the heart." Where is your heart? We must constantly remind ourselves that it's not all about me—my comfort, my status, or my enjoyment. The Bible says that we all are on the earth for a reason, and it not one that is self-centered. Rather, it is Christ centered. If the decisions you make are all about you, you will be missing out on great blessings that God has in store for you. Blessings come by seeking God's plan for your life and doing His will instead of your own will. In the Lord's Prayer, it says, "Thy will be done, on earth as it is in heaven" (Matthew 6:9–13). Making decisions that are Christ centered and others focused may result in less comfort, less status, less fun, but the Bible assures us that our lives will have far more meaning and fulfillment if we do.

Making decisions can be challenging, even agonizing, especially when we act on our own. But know that God wants to be involved in every aspect of our lives, including our decisions, however big or small. He does not promise that there will be easy or quick answers, but He does promise to listen and to guide us—in His way and His timing. We can always be confident of our decisions if we bring the matters before Him. What God did for those Bible characters who sought His wisdom He will surely do for us.

LEADING OTHERS

Leaders are everywhere in every society and at every level. They are found at home, in local communities, and within businesses, governments, schools, sports teams, hospitals, and the military. Countless book, seminars, and other helps on leadership are available to assist people in developing their leadership skills. There is one book on leadership, though, that is often overlooked—the Bible. We may not think of it as a book on leadership, but it is. In fact, it is an excellent guide for leaders in all walks of life. In it are all the essential leadership principles (some of which may surprise you), plus many wonderful examples on how to lead effectively. In this section, we will cover two broad areas of leadership taught in the Bible—what leaders are and what leaders do.

What Leaders Are

Leaders Are Humble

A list of traits commonly associated with leaders usually includes things such as inspires others, driven, self-confident, decisive, communicates well, creates a vision, and the like. Humility is an unlikely addition to the list, yet it is prominent in the Bible. For example, in Numbers 12:3, we read, "Now Moses was a very humble man, more humble than anyone else on the face of the earth"(NIV). Moses was a great leader who led the entire nation of Israel for over forty years. He faced some of the most difficult circumstances any leader could ever experience, such as conflict, disobedience, war, complaining, and food and water shortages. His humility enabled him to be an effective leader of the Israelites all those years for three important reasons. First, by being humble, he was teachable. A proud spirit is one that relies on one's self and inhibits the learning process. This makes it difficult for God (who knows infinitely more than any human) to impart His wisdom and knowledge. This is why scripture says in James 4:6, "God opposes the proud but gives grace to the humble." And again in 1 Peter 5:5–6, we read, "In the same way, younger men, be subject to the elders, and all of you, clothe yourselves with humility toward one another, because God opposes the proud, but gives grace to the humble. Humble yourselves therefore under the mighty hand of God, so that he may exalt you at the right time." God needed to teach Moses many things in order for him to lead an entire nation through the wilderness. Second, and closely related to the first, is that a humble spirit turns to God rather than self or others for help. This enabled Moses to have complete trust in God. Trust is exactly what God desires. One can be a leader without God, but only with God's help can he or she realize their full leadership potential. Reliance on His wisdom and power enables us to be at our best, the kind of leader God wants us to be. Through Him we can accomplish His purposes by leading others effectively. In Philippians 2:3, we read, "Do nothing out of selfish ambition or conceit." If we lead to build ourselves up, we miss what leadership is about. Third, Moses was well prepared to lead. The first eighty years of his life were spent in training. He spent the first forty years living in the house of Pharaoh and no doubt learned academic skills as well as many lessons in leadership. He spent the next forty years tending sheep, where he learned many lessons, such as patience and responsibility. Those experiences prepared him to deal with the many severe challenges he faced while leading his people through the wilderness. But ultimately, it was God who prepared Moses for leadership. God provided the necessary people, gifts, abilities, and experiences that enabled Moses to succeed.

Another example of humility is John the Baptizer who was the forerunner of Jesus. Even though he became well known in the region and had many followers, he understood his purpose and role. One day when he was baptizing members of a crowd, he saw Jesus and immediately addressed Him as the "Lamb of God," a special title reserved for the Son of God. He showed great respect for Jesus when John said he was unworthy even to untie Jesus's sandals. John was a popular leader, but his aspirations were not for status but for serving God. When many of John's disciples left him to follow Jesus, he did not become jealous or angry; rather, he said in John 3:30, "He must increase, but I must decrease." This is one of the most remarkable statements in the Bible and demonstrates a true spirit of humility. John understood and was content with his role and purpose.

We see many other leaders who exhibited humility in scripture. Noah, Job, Daniel, and Paul, to name a few, all demonstrated humility in unique ways. Of course, our chief example of humility is Jesus Christ. Jesus humbled Himself greatly by coming to earth under lowly circumstances. Imagine, a King of kings, who has all authority in this world, born in a stable. During His ministry, Jesus had no possessions, status, or wealth, and yet people followed Him in great numbers. There were no plaques, streets, buildings, or companies bearing his name, and yet following His death and resurrection, the world was changed forever. Jesus led His disciples for several years and still leads followers today. Vast numbers of believers around the world claim Jesus as their Lord and Savior; He is their shepherd leader.

The apostle Peter taught that leaders must not domineer but rather consider themselves as shepherds who care for and serve those whom they lead. This requires humility. Peter clearly expressed this in 1 Peter 5:1–5:

So I exhort the elders among you, as a fellow elder and a witness of the sufferings of Christ, as well as a partaker in the glory that is going to be revealed: shepherd the flock of God that is among you, exercising oversight, not under compulsion, but willingly, as God would have you; not for shameful gain, but eagerly; not domineering over those in your charge, but being examples to the flock. And when the chief Shepherd appears, you will receive the unfading crown of glory. Likewise, you who are younger, be subject to the elders. Clothe yourselves, all of you, with humility toward one another, for God opposes the proud but gives grace to the humble.

Leaders Are Servants

The term *servant* is another leadership trait that doesn't make the top-ten lists. And yet a leader who serves others is one who truly leads. It refers to someone who is at the service of or employed by another person. How can one serve and lead at the same time? Consider Jesus Christ. His entire life (and death) was defined by service. He came on earth for us—for our salvation and to be with Him in eternity. And in Mark 10:42–45, we read, "And Jesus called them to him and said to them, 'You know that those who are considered rulers of the Gentiles lord it over them, and their great ones exercise authority over them. But it shall not be so among you. But whoever would be great among you must be your servant, and whoever would be first among you must be slave of all. For even the Son of Man came not to be served but to serve, and to give his life as a ransom for many.'" Leaders should not use their position of power to domineer over those under them. And in Luke 22:26, Jesus taught "But not so with you. Rather, let the greatest among you become as the youngest, and the leader as one who serves." And similarly, in Matthew 20:26, Jesus said, "It shall not be so among you. But whoever would be great among you must be your servant." Servant leaders are truly great in the eyes of God.

What Leaders Do

Lead with Integrity

A leader always does the right thing, sometimes at great cost. They do not compromise their values, no matter what (see Nehemiah 13:8–24). A leader with integrity realizes that one compromise leads to another and stands firm. Their obedience and allegiance are to God, not popular opinion or culture. They resolve—ahead of time—to resist temptation and affirm that the ends *never* justify the means, if not done with integrity (Nehemiah chapter 5).

In Proverbs 29:12, we read, "If a ruler listens to falsehood, all his officials will be wicked." *Character is key!* Perhaps these standards seem too lofty, but many leaders have exhibited exemplary integrity. Nehemiah is one such leader. The book of Nehemiah is one of the greatest examples of leadership in all of ancient and modern literature. Nehemiah modeled integrity for all generations. When Nehemiah approached King Artaxerxes, there was a level of trust and credibility that can only have been built through years of faithful service. And as his work throughout the book reveals, he was a man of high integrity and character. Everyone wants the big job, but without the character to match it, that big job becomes a curse. Character develops over time as we grow in Christ and weather hardships in His service. A big task plus a weak character usually equals big trouble.

Nehemiah set high standards not only for himself but for those around him as well. He was infuriated by the unjust treatment of people in Israel. He was involved in an important task, but the importance of that task did not justify injustice. People could not be sacrificed in the pursuit of the project.

When evil or injustice is discovered, leaders identify the issue and deal with it quickly. They confront the wrongdoers and troublemakers immediately and deal with them decisively. Nehemiah learned of injustices that were being done by the local leaders in Jerusalem. Nehemiah discerned what the issue was and confronted those leaders directly.

Below are some additional passages that illustrate the importance of integrity:

> Moreover, look for able men from all the people, men who fear God, who are trustworthy and hate a bribe, and place such men over the people as chiefs of thousands, of hundreds, of fifties, and of tens. (Exodus 18:21)

> A ruler who lacks understanding is a cruel oppressor, but he who hates unjust gain will prolong his days. (Proverbs 28:16)

> By justice a king builds up the land, but he who exacts gifts tears it down. (Proverbs 29:4)

> Do your best to present yourself to God as one approved, a worker who has no need to be ashamed, rightly handling the word of truth. (2 Timothy 2:15)

Lead by Example

Be a role model for all those around you (Nehemiah 4:23, Nehemiah 5:9–10; 14–16; 10:1). Great leaders are examples to others. They walk the talk. There are many wonderful role models in the Bible—Abraham, Moses, Esther, Noah, David, Isaiah, John the Baptizer, Peter, Mary, Paul, and many more. These men and women provide a standard for conduct for all of us. They were not perfect but lived their lives to please God rather than men. Jesus is of course our ultimate role model. For those of us who choose to be called followers of Jesus, we continually strive to be like Him in every way. That is the gold standard for leadership—when followers strive to imitate a leader. Peter said it well in 1 Peter 5:3, "Not domineering over those in your charge, but being examples to the flock."

Seek Wise Counsel

Good leaders never go it alone. They seek people who they trust and who will provide sound advice. In Proverbs 15:22, it says, "Plans fail for lack of counsel, but with many advisers they succeed." And similarly, in Proverbs 12:15, it says, "The way of fools seems right to them, but the wise listen to advice." There are two components here to seeking wise counsel. First, one must recognize individuals with wisdom. Second, one must recognize and accept wise counsel. Both are equally important.

Pray

We see this with Nehemiah. He was a man of prayer (Nehemiah 1:4–11) and continually sought God's power and presence through prayer. Since God's work can only be accomplished by His power, seeking Him and bringing the big as well as the small challenges to Him is essential. Nehemiah's prayers included adoration of God, recognizing who He is, a plea for help, a confession, a reminder of God's promises, and a request for blessings/favor. Men and women of prayer recognize that their leadership depends on God's leadership.

Plan

Good leaders make plans. These are not necessarily detailed, elaborate, or even written, but they take time to think through a course of action. An example of this is found in Nehemiah 2:11–16. When Nehemiah first arrived in Jerusalem, he made a careful, private exploration of the problem—the broken down walls of the city. He took the time to evaluate the status and formulate a plan. God blessed his plans, and they were successful.

Motivate Others

Nehemiah could never have accomplished the rebuilding of the wall around Jerusalem without mobilizing a team. Together they accomplished an amazing feat. His team, however, was not comprised of laborers who were skilled in stone masonry or in the art of building city gates. Almost none of them were. Nehemiah chapter 3 indicates that they were goldsmiths (3:8), perfume makers, merchants (3:32), daughters (3:12), and the like. Nehemiah did not order the people to work, nor did he have the money to pay wages. What did he do then that resulted in an entire city getting behind an enormous project while facing opposition? He did three important things. First, he presented the problem but also provided the vision and reason for rebuilding the wall, which they could all relate to. He involved the people and got their buy-in. Second, Nehemiah presented a plan for accomplishing the task. Everyone was organized into a work team. Third, he submitted his plan to God and asked Him for help in carrying this out. And God answered his prayer. The people agreed wholeheartedly to stop everything they were doing and became united in purpose. Nehemiah challenged the people, and they responded. They understood the why, what, and the how of the project. Successful leaders motivate others and are careful to give credit to them for what they have done. Here is the real key though. If you operate on God's agenda, He does the convicting and convincing. You do not have to manipulate, pressure, bully, or intimidate anyone to agree with you. If you are on God's agenda, then God is behind it and will motivate and guide

Love and Care about Those Whom They Lead

Great leaders do today what great leaders did during biblical times; they genuinely care about those they lead, whether in a church, at home, in government, in business, or any other situation. Those who do discover a commitment by those they lead like none other and are greatly rewarded for their efforts. It may be possible to lead without caring about those you lead, but it is far more rewarding and effective if the leaders have genuine love and concern for those under their authority. This is true for Nehemiah, whose leadership abilities are documented by the book with his name. The walls of Jerusalem had been broken down and its gates burned; the city was in ruins. Nehemiah understood the situation of the residents perhaps better than even they did—the walls represented a disgrace because it showed everyone that God had rejected the people because of their sins. It also left them unprotected. Too, Nehemiah saw the poor and oppressed in the city, and his heart was broken (Nehemiah 5:1–11). Nehemiah was genuinely concerned for the people and made a commitment to change their situation and restore honor to the people and their city. The citizens evidently recognized his concern and responded with overwhelming support.

Throughout Jesus's ministry, we see genuine care and love for His twelve disciples and everyone else. For example, in Mark 6:34, it says, "When Jesus landed and saw a large crowd, he had compassion on them, because they were like sheep without a shepherd. So he began teaching them many things." Compassion defined Jesus's ministry. Elsewhere, we read in 1 Peter 5:7, "Cast all your anxiety on Him because He cares for you." In Matthew 11:28–30, Jesus said, "Come to me, all you who are weary and burdened, and I will give you rest. Take my yoke upon you and learn from me, for I am gentle and humble in heart, and you will find rest for your souls. For my yoke is easy and my burden is light." Jesus loved all those who came to Him then, and He loves us today. He genuinely cares about each one of us more than we can ever imagine. He understands all of life's trials and tribulations and wants to help us through each one we face. Similarly, we too must show genuine concern for others, especially those we lead. It makes all the difference.

Persevere

Great leaders expect opposition and obstacles. They recognize that these come with leadership. But rather than being afraid or intimidated, they confront them openly and quickly. Sometimes the opposition is big and powerful, but they face it with courage. They refuse to quit. More importantly, great leaders expect the power of God to overcome obstacles. Continuing with Nehemiah as an example, we see how he confronted those who opposed and even threatened him. In Nehemiah chapters 4–6, Nehemiah relied on God's involvement and strength in the rebuilding process to pave the way for success. Two individuals, Sanballat and Tobiah, were opposed to the rebuilding of the wall and were determined to thwart this project. They began by trying to convince Nehemiah and the people to give up. After seeing that this did not deter them, they wrote a letter to King Artexerxes containing false information to put an end to the wall project. Nehemiah was undaunted. They then threatened to attack the city to end the work. Nehemiah responded by directing half of the workers to perform guard duty while the others worked. Nehemiah even overcame the apathy of some of the people in Jerusalem who refused to help. God wants to be involved in every aspect of our plans, and if asked, He will always do what is needed when it is needed. As a result, the wall was completed in an astonishing fifty-two days. Nehemiah and the people saw the project through to completion, in spite of many obstacles (Nehemiah 2:9–10; 4:1–10).

Jesus faced opposition throughout His ministry but persevered through it all. The temple leaders opposed Jesus bitterly and time after time attempted to trap Him so that He could be arrested. Jesus had a mission to accomplish, and nothing could deter Him. We can only imagine how painful it was for Jesus, the Savior of the world, to be hated and rejected by men. Nevertheless, Jesus faithfully and obediently remained focused on His mission, even though it meant great suffering and death. He understood His greater purpose. That's what great leaders do; they persevere.

Develop Others

Effective leaders help their employees be the best they can be at whatever they do. They develop and support those whom they lead so that they reach their full potential. They treat their employees with respect and expect the best from them. Jesus provided the perfect example of this. He spent several years teaching and developing His disciples. The end result was that they became highly effective leaders of the early church throughout the Middle East. Leaders who develop others foster loyalty and commitment, which enables the success of that leader. We reap what we sow!

The Bible, then, is an excellent book on leadership. In it are contained all the essential principles of leadership, which can be applied at all levels and all areas of life. This should not be surprising because God is the perfect example, and He created us in His image.

PLANNING

Whether they are formal or informal, written or unwritten, accomplishments normally begin with a plan. It may be as broad as one's entire life or a master development plan, or as specific as a short-term plan for business, a sports team, school, construction project, or planting crop. Workers plan for retirement, students plan their careers, brides and grooms plan their weddings, businesses plan for future growth, engineers develop detailed project plans, and travelers plan a route. To achieve one's destination, planning is crucial. This is true for every walk of life and every stage of life.

At first, one might think this topic is beyond the realm of the Bible. Instead, we find it prominent throughout, complete with excellent examples of planning by various characters. This should be expected because the master of planning is God Himself. He planned life itself down to the tiniest details—the earth with all its complexities, earth's solar system, our galaxy, and beyond. By His divine hand, He made (and executed) a perfect plan for the salvation of humankind. Moreover, God continues to plan today. He has plans for individuals, families, and entire nations. As revealed in Jeremiah 29:11, "For I know the plans I have for you, declares the Lord, plans to prosper and not harm you, plans to give you hope and a future." God plans the bigger picture as well as details.

There are many Bible characters who provide wonderful illustrations of planning, including Noah, who worked on a decades-long ark-building project (the details of which were provided directly by God); Solomon, who built a magnificent temple; Nehemiah, who rebuilt the Jerusalem walls and gates; Ezra, who rebuilt the temple after it was destroyed; and Paul, who planned multiple church-planting journeys. Many other examples could be cited for plans that were made for battles, for travel, for planting, for building, and more. There are several key principles that the Bible teaches us about planning.

Develop the Plan

Proverbs 21:5 says, "The plans of the diligent lead to profit as surely as haste leads to poverty." And Proverbs 20:4 says, "A sluggard does not plow in season; so at harvest time he looks but finds nothing." If we don't plan, we cannot achieve. Further, we must plan and then act on that plan. When he first learned of the state of affairs in Jerusalem, Nehemiah developed a plan to repair the wall. He did not understand all that needed to be done at first but developed the framework for completing the task. As he learned more, Nehemiah filled in the details of how the work would be accomplished. He planned and then followed through on his plan. When entering the land of Canaan, Joshua made plans for organizing the twelve tribes into fighting units and made plans for various battles.

In Isaiah 32:8, it says, "But the noble man makes noble plans, and by noble deeds he stands." In other words, the person who is honorable makes honorable plans and stands behind what he does. He is trustworthy. To put it simply, say what you are going to do and do what you say.

Seek Advice

It is wise to seek input from trusted advisers. In Proverbs 15:22, it says, "Plans fail for lack of counsel, but with many advisers they succeed." They can help you avoid mistakes and make wise choices. This applies to all types of plans. In Proverbs 20:18, we read, "Make plans by seeking advice; if you wage war, obtain guidance." Whether for education, business, military encounters, government, or household matters, ask for input. Two of the reasons why someone might not seek counsel are because of pride or because of the lack of understanding (don't know what they don't know). In either case, failure is far more likely when we develop plans in isolation. The best plans withstand the scrutiny of knowledgeable advisers.

Involve God in the Plan

God desires to be involved with our plans, even the smallest ones. When Nehemiah developed his plans to rebuild the wall, he asked for guidance from God. Nehemiah did not understand all of the how, but God did. The following three proverbs illustrate this point:

> Commit to the LORD whatever you do, and your plans will succeed. (Proverbs 16:3)

> In his heart a man plans his course, but the LORD determines his steps. (Proverbs 16:9)

> To man belong the plans of the heart, but from the LORD comes the reply of the tongue. (Proverbs 16:1)

Notice in the first passage it says, "whatever you do." Through experience, I have learned that God is interested in the smallest of details of a plan—even things that I thought would not be worth His time. But He wants to be part of both the big and small plans; He wants to see us succeed in all that we do. Isn't that wonderful? That the God of the universe cares about every aspect of our lives! If we ask for God's input through prayer, He will respond. It may be through ideas, inspirations, advisers, or other means, but He will answer. This is because He loves us and cares for us and desires to bless us. In Psalm 20:4, it says, "May he give you the desire of your heart and make all your plans succeed." If you ask, He will help. He will guide us toward good choices and away from mistakes. After all, God sees the future, and we cannot.

Seek God's Plans for You

Did you know that God has plans for each one of us? In Proverbs 33:1, it says, "But the plans of the LORD stand firm forever, the purposes of his heart through all generations." And as referred to earlier, Proverbs 19:21 says, "Many are the plans in a man's heart, but it is the LORD's purpose that prevails." There are things that God wants accomplished in this world, and He desires to use us for His purposes. A wonderful example of this involves the prophet Moses. God purposed that the descendants of Jacob would be freed from bondage and led to Canaan. God planned how they were to be released and also planned their escape route. God chose Moses to lead the nation, and He had prepared Moses to do this from his infancy. Moses may have had other plans, but eventually he aligned his plans with God's plans, and this made all the difference. God used Moses and blessed him greatly. God wants us to plan but also desires that we align our plans with His plans. This is accomplished through prayer. Ask God what He desires for you. Then your plans will belong to Him, and you too will be greatly blessed.

WISDOM FOR WORK

Work is defined as the exertion of effort to produce or accomplish something. It can be physical or mental and in many different forms. We sometimes refer to it as labor or toil and often in terms of one's occupation or career. But it can be any situation in which effort is involved. From the very first verses in the Bible, we learn something about work. God worked by creating the universe and everything therein. God's creative work was followed by pauses to reflect upon His handiwork, and after each creation period, it says, "And God saw everything that he had made, and behold, it was very good" (Genesis 1:31). But God's work did not end there. He has continued to work throughout history, though in different ways. He performed miracles, such as the ten plagues in Egypt, and He acted in the lives of people, such as Abraham and Noah and through His prophets. Throughout the Bible, there is a long list of deeds that God performed including providing food and water, performing signs and wonders, and defeating entire armies. In Psalm 145:6, the psalmist speaks about it this way: "They will tell of the power of your awesome works and I will proclaim your great deeds" (NIV). God continues to work today throughout the world by working in and through people. He does this through the Holy Spirit, who, though invisible to us, is hard at work everywhere. We know this because we can see the fruit of His work in people and events.

It was God's intent from the beginning that work be an integral part of our lives. As God began to teach Adam, we read in Genesis 2:15, "The LORD God took the man and put him in the Garden of Eden to work it and keep it." The concept of work comes directly from God, and we are expected to work. The Bible teaches that not only are we expected to work, but also our attitude toward work is important. The apostle Paul made this comment about work: "Whatever you do, work at it with all your heart, as working for the Lord, not for human masters" (Colossians 3:23). Paul added this comment as well in 1 Corinthians 10:31, "So, whether you eat or drink, or whatever you do, do all to the glory of God." How can this be when there are many kinds of work that are extremely difficult or boring or mentally and/or physically exhausting? How can God be honored and glorified by our work? There are several important ways. We honor God By maintaining a positive attitude toward work. As just mentioned, work is something that God has ordained and expects of us. When we work, it is a form of obedience to God. Second, the attitude that we bring to our work can be an influence on others—negatively or positively. When we do our work cheerfully and to the best of our ability, we can point others to God. Third, we honor God by showing proper respect to those in authority over our work. This, too, demonstrates the love of Jesus in our hearts. Fourth, when we work honestly and faithfully, it demonstrates integrity and is a reflection of our moral character. Lastly, it honors God when we use the gifts and abilities He Himself has given us to accomplish meaningful things. Similarly, wasting our talents displeases Him.

Doing all these things (and no doubt others could be added) brings glory to God. We do our best because God expects our best. And work performed with the right attitude and approach is pleasing to God. In 2 Corinthians 6:5, the apostle Paul recognized that work may sometimes be quite difficult and challenging. Paul also stressed that we must work willingly. In 1 Thessalonians 3:10, he writes, "For even when we were with you, we gave you this rule: The one who is unwilling to work shall not eat." These are pretty strong words about the importance of work. Clearly, whatever we have, we should earn it through work. In Revelation 2:2, we see another reference to hard work in which Jesus acknowledges the work and perseverance of the church in Ephesus. Hard work includes perseverance; we must stick with it until it is completed. Jesus Himself reflected on the reason why He came to earth. In John 17:4, Jesus said, "I glorified you on earth, having accomplished the work that you gave me to do." Jesus did His work here on earth willingly, persistently, and with love—for us—even though it was unimaginably difficult.

There are many other examples of work throughout the Bible, but some of the most profound insights are found in the book of Proverbs. Approximately thirty verses relate to work and offer great advice for us. Wisdom about work can broadly be arranged into two categories: the benefits of hard work and the evils of laziness. Here are some examples:

> Lazy hands make a man poor but diligent hands bring wealth. (Proverbs 10:4)

> He who gathers crops in summer is a wise son, but he who sleeps during harvest is a disgraceful son. (Proverbs 10:5)

> All hard work brings a profit, but mere talk leads only to poverty. (Proverbs 14:23)

> In all toil there is profit, but mere talk tends only to poverty. (Proverbs 14:23)

Commit your work to the LORD, and your plans will be established. (Proverbs 16:3)

Do you see a man skilled in his work? He will serve before kings; he will not serve before obscure men. (Proverbs 22:20)

These passages teach us that we are to do our best at whatever work is before us, that work is not only beneficial but brings honor to those in authority, and that hard work should be done with excellence. Rather than work being mere drudgery and distasteful, our attitude should be to do whatever work is available to us in a positive way and do our best. In Psalm 90:17, the psalmist prayed, "Let the favor of the Lord our God be upon us, and establish the work of our hands upon us; yes, establish the work of our hands!" This is a wonderful reminder that for all work, we should ask for God's favor on what we do. It is critically important to have God's favor on our work.

The Bible has warnings for those who are not willing to work. Consider the following scripture passages:

Go to the ant, O sluggard; consider her ways, and be wise. Without having any chief, officer, or ruler, she prepares her bread in summer and gathers her food in harvest. (Proverbs 6:6–8)

A slack hand causes poverty, but the hand of the diligent makes rich. (Proverbs 10:4)

He who gathers in summer is a prudent son, but he who sleeps in harvest is a son who brings shame. (Proverbs 10:5)

Whoever works his land will have plenty of bread, but he who follows worthless pursuits lacks sense. (Proverbs 12:11)

In all toil there is profit, but mere talk tends only to poverty. (Proverbs 14:23)

Whoever is slack in his work is a brother to him who destroys. (Proverbs 18:9)

I passed by the field of a sluggard, by the vineyard of a man lacking sense, and behold, it was all overgrown with thorns; the ground was covered with nettles, and its stone wall was broken down. Then I saw and considered it; I looked and received instruction. A little sleep, a little slumber, a little folding of the hands to rest, and poverty will come upon you like a robber, and want like an armed man. (Proverbs 24:30–34)

From these verses, we see that there is a clear difference between those who are willing to work and those who are not. Those who are lazy will suffer the consequences—which may include poverty and hunger.

Not only does work bring many practical benefits, such as providing income for food, clothing, and housing, but it has the added benefit of blessings from God, as illustrated in the following passages:

Have you not put a hedge around him and his house and all that he has, on every side? You have blessed the work of his hands, and his possessions have increased in the land. (Job 1:10)

You shall eat the fruit of the labor of your hands; you shall be blessed, and it shall be well with you. (Psalm 128:2)

The soul of the sluggard craves and gets nothing, while the soul of the diligent is richly supplied. (Proverbs 13:4)

Do you see a man skillful in his work? He will stand before kings; he will not stand before obscure men. (Proverbs 22:29)

The Bible is clear. We are expected to work, and whatever work we do, we are to do it to the honor and glory of God. God notices our work and is pleased when we do our best to honor Him.

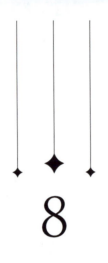

8

LIVING IN COMMUNITY

A new commandment I give to you, that you love one another:
just as I have loved you, you also are to love one another.
—John 13:34

We were made for community. God intended that we live in close
contact with others in families, neighborhoods, and villages and
beyond. This includes the church, where we are intended to live in close
fellowship with one another, as a family. When living in community, we
learn how to implement all practical applications mentioned earlier as well
as those that follow. It is difficult if not impossible to learn how to love
and show kindness or compassion if we exist in isolation; that is not God's
desire. And there is so much to be learned from one another. Community
is a wonderful training ground for developing character and learning life
lessons that God intended for us. Community is critically important for
us to reach our potential. And it is the Bible that provides the instruction
for successful community life.

BEAR ONE ANOTHER'S BURDENS

The world we live in is full of challenges, and it has been this way ever since
the beginning. Each day can bring its own set of new troubles. At times,
these challenges can become heavy burdens that are difficult to bear. This
is especially true if we attempt to carry these alone.

A burden is anything that oppresses a person, or something that makes an overwhelming demand, or something that brings sorrow or grief. Some examples follow:

- physical—a lingering health issue or disability
- financial—lack of or loss of income or heavy debt
- emotional—stress at home or work from relationships
- disappointment—with people or circumstances
- care for others—being a care provider for someone
- failure—failing ourselves or others
- injustice—either to ourselves or others
- sin—guilt or shame from something we did

What are we to do with these burdens when they are too heavy for us to bear alone? Actually, according to the Bible, we are not expected to bear these by ourselves. It is God's design that burdens be shared. There are two critically important avenues of help—from God and from those around us. Living in community enables us to bear our loads with family, friends, and neighbors—with God's help.

God understands burdens completely and invites us to bring them to Him in prayer. Psalm 55:22 says, "Cast your burden on the LORD, and he will sustain you; he will never permit the righteous to be moved." And in Psalm 68:19, it says: "Praise be to the Lord, to God our Savior, who daily bears our burdens." Note the word *daily*; we cannot overwhelm God with our burdens, nor will He grow weary from hearing about our troubles. Moreover, there is no burden too large for Him to bear. In Matthew 11:28, Jesus said, "Come to me, all you who are weary and burdened, and I will give you rest." Jesus welcomes our burdens, all kinds of burdens. And in the next verse, Jesus says, "Take my yoke upon you and learn from me, for I am gentle and humble in heart, and you will find rest for your souls." When we bring these to God, we can be sure that He listens and that He will truly carry our burdens. We simply explain to God what is on our heart, and He promises to listen. But it doesn't stop there; He also promises to help us. How He does this depends on each situation. It may be through inspirations, encouragement, other people, or circumstances, but we can be sure that He will be there for us and that we can fully trust Him.

In Galatians 6:2, the apostle Paul wrote, "Bear one other's burdens, and so fulfill the law of Christ." We are expected to help carry the burdens of family, friends, and neighbors. By doing so, we demonstrate, in practical ways, the command to love our neighbors as ourselves (Mark 12:30–31). It is God's intent that we help each other. Helping carry someone's burdens may not be easy and can require sacrifice. It also means that we do something—take action. There are many ways to show love to others and help carry their burdens. We do this by praying for them and providing physical and/or emotional support, whatever that may be. We listen carefully so that we can fully understand their situation and either provide the required help or find ways to get the help they need. The goal is complete restoration. If someone is struggling under a load, we help carry the load; if someone falls down, we lift them back up. By carrying each other's burdens, we do what Jesus would want us to do.

There are many examples in the Bible of burdens being carried by others. The Old Testament character Job was comforted by friends who sat silent with him for many days. Naomi was helped by her daughter-in-law, who cared for her and helped her through the loss of her husband and two sons. Moses was burdened by his people, who were often complaining or even rebelling, but God answered his requests for help. And King David, who committed a grievous sin, in Psalm 32, he described how he was groaning under the weight of the guilt he felt. Later, in the same psalm (38:4), David wrote, "My guilt has overwhelmed me like a burden too heavy to bear." But David took this burden to God in prayer, and God forgave and released him from his guilt. David could not bear the weight of his burden alone, and neither can we. When we talk to God about our burdens, we acknowledge the burden and trust that God will help carry that burden.

However great our burdens might be, they should not be our focus and consume us. God's desire is that we live a life of victory, not defeat. His desire is that we focus on Him and serve Him to the very best of our abilities. God wants us to experience joy in our lives. Jesus was keenly aware of the needs of those around Him. He healed the sick, the lame could walk, and the blind could see, which encouraged those carrying burdens. The Bible tells us to set our minds on things above, not things on earth—to keep our focus on Jesus, not things of this world (Colossians 3:1–2). One of the ways we can do this is to literally count our blessings. List the good things that God has provided and done for you. Another way is to focus on the needs of others. Almost always, there is someone you know who has burdens and needs help. An ancillary benefit is that by helping others, one's own burdens often seem less important.

There may be situations when burdens remain in our lives and we wonder if God is listening or cares. We must be aware, however, that this may be God's way of teaching us important truths or lessons. The apostle Paul was burdened by a something he described as a "thorn in the flesh" (2 Corinthians 12:7), but God did not take it away from him. It continually reminded Paul that His grace was sufficient for him. Paul was also burdened by a deep sorrow for his fellow Israelites (Romans 9:1–9) who had not accepted the gospel. This burden drove Paul to do his best to spread the gospel wherever he went. Paul accepted his burdens, and with God's help, he remained effective in his work. These kinds of burdens may be difficult for us to understand. It isn't that God does not care. Rather, He cares deeply but may have some greater purpose in mind. We accept God's wisdom in all matters—the pleasant and painful alike. But Paul had many who helped carry his burdens. They did this through words of encouragement, prayer, physical help, and acts of kindness. Paul was loved by God and his friends, and this made burdens feel light to him. And that, friends, is true for us too!

ENCOURAGING OTHERS

One of Satan's goals is to tear people down. He is delighted when people feel discouraged, filled with doubt, powerless, and ineffective. He constantly lies to us by telling us that we have little value or, even worse, we are worthless. The Bible tells us that Satan is the father of lies (John 8:44). Most of us feel discouraged at times and may even question our self-worth. One of the best antidotes for these feelings is encouragement. To encourage someone means to build them up, give them confidence and hope, so that they are able to accomplish all that lies before them and lead fulfilled lives. All of us need encouragement, sometimes daily, and there is a risk that discouragement persists or reappears. The result can be that we live a defeated life in which there is little hope and without our joy in Christ.

There are a number of passages in the Bible that instruct (command) us to encourage one another. In 1 Thessalonians 5:11, we read, "Therefore encourage one another and build one another up, just as you are doing." Hebrews 3:13 says, "But encourage one-another daily" (NIV). In Acts 15:32, Judas and Silas said much to encourage and strengthen the brothers. And in Acts 20:1–2, it says, "Paul sent for the disciples and, after encouraging them, said farewell and set out for Macedonia. When he had gone through those regions and had given much encouragement, he came to Greece." Regular encouragement was integral to the life of the early church. In fact, Paul mentions in Romans 12:8 that encouragement is a spiritual gift that is to be used for the benefit of others. Our role is to build others up, never the opposite. It is for their benefit.

How then should we encourage one another? In the Bible, we see encouragement accomplished by both words and actions. The words we choose can encourage in significant ways. They can build up, affirm, and demonstrate that you care. Sometimes our words make a dramatic difference in the lives of others by instilling confidence, inspiring, and motivating. They can also strengthen someone, as mentioned in Deuteronomy 32:28 and Acts 15:32. Encouraging words can not only lift spirits but also spur people on to action. We see this in the Old Testament, where leaders were encouraged before a battle, and in the New Testament, they were encouraged to persevere. When Moses was near the end of his life, he provided encouragement to his successor, Joshua. In Deuteronomy 31:7–8, it says, "Then Moses summoned Joshua and said to him in the sight of all of Israel, 'Be strong and courageous, for you shall go with this people into the land that the Lord has sworn to their fathers to give them, and you shall put them in possession of it. It is the Lord who goes before you. He will be with you; He will not leave you or forsake you. Do not fear or be dismayed.'" Imagine how much this helped Joshua during his conquest of the Promised Land (Canaan) as he faced great challenges not only from his enemies but from those he was leading. Finally, in Acts 16:40, we see one more example of encouragement. "After Paul and Silas came out of the prison, they went to Lydia's house, where they met with the brothers and encouraged them. Then they left." Notice that even though Paul and Silas had just left prison, they were already encouraging others. Even while in prison, Paul encouraged his brother, Timothy. They did not dwell on their own situation but rather found the strength to build up others. Paul cared so much about his brothers that he often overlooked his own situation.

The Bible teaches that we can also encourage others by our actions. Doing things with, doing things for, being present, listening, and asking questions are all things that can be done to encourage others. For instance, in Paul's letter to Philemon, in verse 7, he said, "Your love has given me great joy and encouragement, because you, brother, have refreshed the hearts of the saints." Our actions can encourage like refreshing water, giving strength and hope to others.

Even circumstances and situations can provide encouragement. In Acts 11:23, we read, "When he [Barnabas] arrived and saw the evidence of the grace of God, he was glad and encouraged them all to remain true to the Lord with all their hearts" (NIV). God provides encouragement to us through things He does. It may be by providing much-needed rain, healing, material things, employment, or any other need that may arise. When we see evidence of God's hand in something, we can take courage and be confident that He is with us.

The Bible contains many other verses that provide encouragement for a variety of situations:

- When afraid, Joshua 1:9 says, "Have I not commanded you? Be strong and courageous. Do not be afraid; do not be discouraged, for the Lord your God will be with you wherever you go."
- When weary, Isaiah 40:31 says, "But those who hope in the Lord will renew their strength. They will soar on wings like eagles; they will run and not grow weary, they will walk and not be faint" (NIV).
- When facing uncertainty, Psalm 31:24 says, "Be strong and let your heart take courage, all you who wait for the Lord."

- When feeling discouraged, Psalm 23:4 says, "Even though I walk through the darkest valley, I will fear no evil, for you are with me; your rod and your staff, they comfort me."
- When searching for answers, Psalm 121:1–2 says, "I lift up my eyes to the mountains—where does my help come from? My help comes from the Lord, who made heaven and earth."
- When burdened, Matthew 11:28 says, "Come to me, all you who are weary and burdened, and I will give you rest" (NIV).
- When feeling worthless, Luke 12:6–7 says, "Are not five sparrows sold for two pennies? Yet not one of them is forgotten by God. Indeed, the very hairs of your head are all numbered. Don't be afraid; you are worth more than many sparrows" (NIV).
- When anxious, John 14:27 says, "Peace I leave with you; my peace I give you. I do not give to you as the world gives. Do not let your hearts be troubled and do not be afraid" (NIV).
- When feeling alone, Romans 8:31 says, "What, then, shall we say to these things? If God is for us, who can be against us."
- When experiencing sorrow, Psalm 34:18 says, "The LORD is close to the brokenhearted; he rescues those whose spirits are crushed" (NLT).

The God of the Bible is a God who loves and provides encouragement for people in all kinds of situations we may encounter. He accomplishes this directly through His Word, through the Holy Spirit, and through circumstances. Often, He chooses to do this through family, friends, and neighbors. We must, therefore, always be alert for opportunities to help others overcome discouragement by building and lifting up one another. This is always to be done in love.

FORGIVING OTHERS

Forgiveness refers to an intentional decision to let go of anger, resentment, or retaliation toward an individual (or group) who has wronged you. This individual or group may or may not deserve your forgiveness, and they may or may not admit fault or apologize for their words or actions. You decide to no longer hold onto negative feelings and say, "I forgive you," either verbally or in your heart and move on. This does not mean that you deny or minimize the offense. For many, forgiving others is difficult. It may even seem impossible for some. We tend to hold on to feelings of anger, resentment, and bitterness rather than putting them behind us.

The Bible explains very clearly both that we must forgive and why we must forgive others. We forgive because God wants and expects us to do so; it is not optional. Put simply, if we cannot forgive others, neither will God forgive us. In Matthew 6:12, Jesus said, "And forgive us our debts, as we also have forgiven our debtors." We are forgiven in accordance to whether we forgive others. In verses 14–15, Jesus further explained this. "For if you forgive other people when they sin against you, your heavenly Father will also forgive you. But if you do not forgive others their sins, your Father will not forgive your sins" (NIV). This is only fair, isn't it? Why would we expect to enjoy forgiveness if we withhold it from others? The apostle Paul instructed us to be kind and compassionate to one another, forgiving each other, just as Christ forgives us. (Ephesians 4:2). Christ forgives us out of His deep love for us, and we are commanded to love and forgive others.

We all do and/or say things that are offensive and hurtful to God. For example, anytime we lie, steal, slander, cheat, lust, idolize something, disobey any commandment, and the like (which may happen frequently), we offend God. God literally hates these things. Even prideful thoughts are offensive to God. But in spite of our shortcomings, God still cares for us and will readily forgive all who are sorry for their sins. This is truly amazing. Even more amazing is that God forgives us over and over for the same sins or new ones that we commit. He does this because of His great mercy and boundless love for people. And He does this for groups of people as well as individuals. Consider the following passages:

> If my people, who are called by my name, will humble
> themselves and pray and seek my face and turn from their
> wicked ways, then I will hear from heaven, and I will forgive
> their sin and will heal their land. (2 Chronicles 7:14)

Then I acknowledged my sin to you and did not cover up my iniquity.
I said, "I will confess my transgressions to the Lord." And you forgave the guilt of my sin. (Psalm 32:5)

Whoever conceals their sins does not prosper, but the one who confesses and renounces them finds mercy. (Proverbs 28:13)

Who is a God like you, who pardons sin and forgives the transgression of the remnant of his inheritance? You do not stay angry forever but delight to show mercy. (Micah 7:18)

Rend your heart and not your garments. Return to the Lord your God, for he is gracious and compassionate, slow to anger and abounding in love, and he relents from sending calamity. (Joel 2:13)

These and other scripture passages teach us that God forgives; mercy and forgiveness are inherent to His nature. God wants us to forgive so that we can be released and set free from our past and live a life of freedom both in the present and future. Like a flowing stream, we are refreshed and renewed by His love and mercy. There is no offense so egregious that will not be forgiven—if confessed. Psalm 103:12 describes God's forgiveness this way: "As far as the east is from the west, so far has he removed our transgressions from us." God is deeply offended by things we do and say, and yet He forgives, and in doing so, He teaches us what true forgiveness is like. When on the cross and suffering agonizing emotional and physical pain at the hands of evil men, Jesus said, "Father, forgive them, for they know not what they do." Jesus understood what it means to forgive, even under the most extreme circumstances. He interceded for His accusers, including those who intensely hated Him. This forgiveness continues on after His death and resurrection. Jesus forgives each person who repents of their sins. Why? Why is it so important to forgive others, even our enemies? The Bible provides many reasons, and we will cover several of these here.

When we forgive others, we are forgiving something that was done or said to us, something that offended or hurt us in some way. Forgiving others is not only expected of us, but God knows that it is what's best for us too. Forgiveness releases and frees us to live and serve joyfully. It also frees us from bitterness and resentment toward those who have offended us, which interferes with our relationship with God. An individual, a family, village, city, or even a nation that cannot forgive may live in a continual cycle of revenge and violence. We must learn to forgive one another; there is no other worthwhile option. For many, the process of letting go can be extremely difficult and take a considerable amount of time. Some are never able to forgive and, sadly, hold on to their negative feelings as long as they live. In fact, the concept of forgiveness is foreign to many throughout the world.

Jesus challenged us to not only forgive others but to do so repeatedly. In Matthew 18:21–22, we find an exchange between Jesus and Peter. "Then Peter came up and said to him, 'Lord, how often will my brother sin against me, and I forgive him? As many as seven times?' Jesus said to him, 'I do not say to you up to seven times, but up to seven times seventy.'" Thus, even if someone offends us a second or third time (or more), we are to continue the process of forgiveness. This was a shocking response for His disciples. But it isn't the number that is so surprising. Rather, it is the idea that forgiveness has no limits. We are to live a lifestyle of forgiveness. As Jesus said in the above passage, it goes on and on. Without forgiveness, we spiral into a life of revenge, bitterness, and even hate. This is, of course, unhealthy for all parties involved.

The Bible teaches us that we must forgive, why we must forgive, and how we must forgive—unconditionally. And we are to do it in love. In fact, forgiveness is an act of love. We forgive regardless of whether the offending person asks for forgiveness. Why then is forgiveness so important to us? Because when we run out of forgiveness, God does too.

HELPING THE POOR

Being poor can be one of the most difficult of life's circumstances. It usually means having limited resources to adequately fulfill basic needs, such as food, clothing, and shelter. Many cannot meet these needs without help. There are many causes of poverty, such as loss of employment, poor health, a disability, exploitation, or loss of a spouse. The Bible mentions the poor often, especially widows and orphans. They are poor due to life circumstances and are particularly vulnerable.

As we consider what the Bible says about this topic, several themes emerge. First is God's deep concern for the poor. This is shown in a summary of the following passages from both the Old and New Testaments:

- Psalm 14:6 says, "The Lord is the refuge of the poor."
- Psalm 35:10 says, "The Lord rescues the poor and needy."
- Psalm 113:7 says, "He raises the poor from the dust and lifts the needy from the ash heap."
- Amos 5:11 says, "God will punish those who trample on the poor."
- Luke 6:20 says, "Blessed are you who are poor, for yours is the kingdom of God."
- Acts 10:4 says, "Your prayers and gifts to the poor are a memorial offering before God."
- James 2:5 says, "God chose the poor in the eyes of the world to be rich in faith."

The poor have a special place in God's heart, and therefore, they must be important to us. Note that the Acts passage provides two specific things we should do: prayers and gifts. We are called to action.

Second, the Bible teaches that we must have a proper attitude toward the poor. Consider the following scripture passages:

- Deuteronomy 15:4 says, "Do not be hardhearted or tightfisted toward the poor."
- Proverbs 17:5 says, "He who mocks the poor shows contempt for their Maker."

- Proverbs 19:17 says, "He who is kind to the poor lends to the LORD."
- Proverbs 22:9 says, "A generous man will be blessed; he shares his food with the poor."
- Acts 9:36 says, "Dorcas was always doing good and helping the poor."

It is easy to blame those who are poor for their situation. But those who have enough must never look down on those who do not or judge them. Rather, we are to show compassion and kindness, just as God does.

Third, God expects those who have resources to help the poor. He commands it, and by doing so, God is pleased and honored. Jesus said, "As you did it to one of the least of these my brothers, you did it to me" (Matthew 25:40). This concept is summarized well in 1 John 3:17, "If anyone has material possessions and sees a brother or sister in need but has no pity on them, how can the love of God be in that person?" (NIV). After all, they are created in His image and are just as special in God's eyes as anyone else. Consider the following scripture passages (as summarized):

- Exodus 23:11 says, "Let the land rest; let the poor harvest the food."
- Leviticus 23:22 says, "Let the poor harvest the edges of the field."
- Leviticus 25:35 says, "If someone becomes poor, help them out."
- Isaiah 58:7 says, "Provide food for the hungry and shelter for the poor."
- Matthew 5:42 says, "Give to the one who begs from you, and do not refuse the one who would borrow from you."
- Luke 14:13 says, "When you give a banquet, invite the poor, crippled, lame, blind."
- Mark 10:21 says, "Sell your possessions and give to the poor."

In Deuteronomy 15:7–8, we read, "If among you, one of your brothers should become poor, in any of your towns within your land that the LORD your God is giving you, you shall not harden your heart or shut your hand against your poor brother, but you shall open your hand to him and lend him sufficient for his need, whatever it may be." Essentially, we give until the need is gone. And in Luke 6:38, it says, "Give, and it will be given to you. Good measure, pressed down, shaken together, running over, will be put into your lap. For with the measure you use it will be measured back to you." The Bible is clear. We are to be generous when it comes to helping the poor. God warns those who ignore the poor and blesses those who help them. Further, consider these blessings and warnings: "Whoever is generous to the poor lends to the Lord, and he will repay him for his deed" (Proverbs 19:17) and "Whoever has a bountiful eye will be blessed, for he shares his bread with the poor" (Proverbs 22:9). And conversely, God opposes those who oppose the poor. "Whoever gives to the poor will not want, but he who hides his eyes will get many a curse" (Proverbs 28:27). Therefore, we must not just talk about the poor but use what God has provided to us to help those in need. When we do, blessings abound.

Fourth, God's concern for the poor includes His desire for justice for the poor. For many reasons, it can be easy to take advantage of the poor. But God says, "Do not do it." This principle is emphasized in the following verses:

- Exodus 23:6 says, "Do not deny justice to your poor people in their lawsuits."
- Deuteronomy 24:14 says, "Do not take advantage of the hired man who is poor or needy."
- Psalm 82:3 says, "Defend the rights of the poor, fatherless, oppressed and destitute."
- Proverbs 13:23 says, "A poor man's field may produce food, but injustice sweeps it away."
- Proverbs 29:7 says, "A righteous man knows the rights of the poor; a wicked man does not understand such knowledge."

We are to not only assure that we treat the poor fairly but also be alert for those who are oppressed by others. Through the prophet Isaiah, God speaks directly to us with these words: "Learn to do good; seek justice, correct oppression; bring justice to the fatherless, plead the widow's cause" (Isaiah 1:17). We must never ignore the poor, regardless of why they are poor, and work toward helping them receive fair treatment.

During Jesus's ministry on earth, He mentioned the poor often. He taught us to live a lifestyle of generosity to those in need. Note in Luke 12:33–34 how important this is to Jesus: "Sell your possessions, and give to the needy. Provide yourselves with moneybags that do not grow old, with a treasure in the heavens that does not fail, where no thief approaches and no moth destroys. For where your treasure is, there will your heart be also." Our level of generosity demonstrates what we treasure—material things or things that matter to God. Jesus also taught us to love others (John 13:34), "A new commandment I give you: Love one another." Love is an action word that requires putting our faith into action. We give and trust that God will provide for us as needed. If we have possessions but do not share with the needy, it is evidence that we do not love others the way that Jesus commanded. And like forgiveness, love is not optional, regardless of their economic status.

LENDING AND BORROWING

Lending and borrowing are everyday practices throughout the world and have been so since ancient times. Entire financial institutions have been established to accommodate the vast demand at the local, regional, and global levels. It is difficult to imagine any society functioning without transactions of this sort. And these range from simple loans to highly complex transactions, and small (micro loans) to vast sums of money. While the Bible does not address even a small fraction of the types of lending and borrowing that occur, it does speak to this very well in the form of risks and responsibilities, which can be generally applied to all levels and types of loans. It provides the principles by which we can all operate.

Lending

Individuals and institutions provide loans for almost anything for individuals, businesses, organizations, corporations, and government agencies. In most situations, loans are made carefully and ethically but not always. Borrowers can be taken advantage of when terms of the loan create burdens for the borrowers. But smaller personal loans still occur with regularity to family members, friends, or neighbors. In either case, the guidelines provided in the Bible make perfect sense. Let us explore some of these here.

The Bible neither prohibits nor encourages lending but does provide guidelines when lending occurs. In Exodus 22:25–27, God spoke these instructions to the prophet Moses: "If you lend money to any of my people with you who are poor, you shall not be like a moneylender to him, and you shall not exact interest from him. If ever you take your neighbor's cloak in pledge, you shall return it to him before the sun goes down, for that is his only covering, and it is his cloak for his body; in what else shall he sleep? And if he cries to me, I will hear, for I am compassionate." Note the last phrase regarding compassion, God expects us to have compassion for those who borrow, just as He does. And according to Deuteronomy 15:7, we are not to withhold help to those in need. It says, "If among you, one of your brothers should become poor, in any of your towns within your land that the LORD your God is giving you, you shall not harden your heart or shut your hand against your poor brother." Compassion for those in need required that the lender not demand interest. Lending was intended to genuinely help others, not be a means of gaining personal wealth at the expense of others. This is repeated in the book of Leviticus (25:37) where it says, "You shall not lend him your money at interest, nor give him your food for profit." And in Ezekiel 18:7–8, we read, "Does not lend at interest or take any profit, withholds his hand from injustice, executes true justice between man and man … Does not oppress anyone, but restores to the debtor his pledge, commits no robbery, gives his bread to the hungry and covers the naked with a garment." Similarly, in the New Testament, Jesus said, "Give to the one who begs from you, and do not refuse the one who would borrow from you" (Matthew 5:42). Lending, then, was intended to be an act of kindness to help those in need. The lesson is this: when you lend, do not take advantage of those who borrow. Lend with a compassionate heart. This does not mean that lenders can never charge interest but that it must not be considered usury in any way.

The above principles were extended to other nations as well.

Deuteronomy 28:12 says, "The LORD will open to you his good treasury, the heavens, to give the rain to your land in its season and to bless all the work of your hands. And you shall lend to many nations, but you shall not borrow." God's blessings to a nation were intended to be a blessing to one's foreign neighbors, but He did not want them to be indebted to others.

One other verse on lending is perhaps surprising. Lending principles were to be extended even to one's enemies. Luke 6:35 says, "But love your enemies, and do good, and lend, expecting nothing in return, and your reward will be great, and you will be sons of the Most High, for he is kind to the ungrateful and the evil." This should not be surprising, though, because God's very nature is love. In the Sermon on the Mount, Jesus taught that we are to love our enemies and pray for those who persecute us (Matthew 5:44). God's standards for compassion and mercy apply to all, regardless of their relationship to us. He extends His grace and mercy to us even though we deserve to be treated as though we were His enemies.

Borrowing

Borrowing comes in many forms, ranging from traditional bank loans, mortgages, and credit cards to personal loans. The Bible does not prohibit borrowing, and there may be legitimate reasons to borrow, such as starting a business or obtaining property or buying goods and services. But the Bible does not encourage borrowing either, and it warns about the dangers of borrowing. In Romans 13:8, the apostle Paul admonished us with these words: "Owe no one anything, except to love each other, for the one who loves another has fulfilled the law."

There are at least four concerns with borrowing and amassing debt. First, when borrowing occurs between friends, neighbors, and family members, it changes the relationship between the lender and borrower. Until repaid, the borrower is indebted to the lender. Proverbs 22:7 says, "The rich rule over the poor, and the borrower is the slave of the lender." The borrower is not free to do as they please with their money; they are obligated to repay their debt first. And Deuteronomy 28:44 says, "He shall lend to you, and you shall not lend to him. He shall be the head, and you shall be the tail." The lender is in control of the relationship.

The second issue with borrowing involves the risk of defaulting on the loan. It may not be possible to repay a debt according to the terms. The borrower may become ill, unemployed, or have other urgent needs that legitimately prevent or delay repayment. This may result in emotional strain on the borrower and his/her family. In ancient times, failure to repay a loan could result in imprisonment of the borrower and/or the children. They might become bond servants until the debt was repaid. Proverbs 22:26–27 says, "Be not one of those who give pledges, who put up security for debts. If you have nothing with which to pay, why should your bed be taken from under you?" And Habakkuk 2:6–7 says, "Shall not all these take up their taunt against him, with scoffing and riddles for him, and say, 'Woe to him who heaps up what is not his own—for how long?—and loads himself with pledges!' Will not your debtors suddenly arise, and those awake who will make you tremble? Then you will be spoil for them." Today, it is not uncommon for individuals to default on loans. The result can be damaging to the borrower's credit and to his/her family.

The third issue with borrowing relates to using one's resources wisely. Loans normally require an interest rate, which can be quite high, meaning that individuals pay a higher total cost for the same goods or services than if they were purchased with cash. That money spent on interest could have been used to help and serve others. Debt-free living is advisable wherever and whenever possible. While loans may be an acceptable choice for many to obtain needed goods or services, they must be done wisely.

Lastly, borrowing may occur in lieu of putting one's trust in God's provision and/or timing. Sometimes borrowing is done so that the goods or services are obtained immediately, when in reality, it is a want and not a need. Too, we may choose to follow our own understanding instead of seeking the wisdom of God. There are many instances in which the things needed were provided without having to borrow money. Thus, there are situations in which one simply needs to trust God to provide. Proverbs 3:5–6 says, "Trust in the Lord with all your heart and lean not on your own understanding. In all your ways acknowledge Him and He will direct your paths." Before you borrow, bring the matter to God and seek His wisdom. God will always guide your plans if you ask Him.

If one does borrow, it should be obvious that the debt must be repaid.

In Psalm 37:21, we read, "The wicked borrows but does not pay back, but the righteous give generously." Borrowing without intent of repayment is stealing and is deeply offensive to God.

When lending and borrowing, it must be remembered that in reality, none of the money actually belongs to us. The Bible teaches that we are simply stewards of what God has given us. God is sovereign, is in control of all things, and owns everything in this world (and universe). Whatever we have, we have because God blesses us with it (whether we acknowledge it or not). Thus, whatever we have, we must manage in a manner that pleases God. And similarly, whatever we need, we must seek the wisdom of He who owns it all.

LOVING ONE ANOTHER

Love for others means having a deliberate feeling of affection or concern for another individual (or individuals). And there is genuine interest in the well-being of the other person. These individuals may be family members, neighbors, or coworkers and can be any age or ethnicity. There are many ways that this word is used, and it is extended to the love of material things, such as food or money. The desire and ability to love is a part of human nature; we were designed with the desire and ability to love. The word *love* occurs in nearly every book of the Bible and 544 times in all. It is a central truth of the Bible. There are three main ways that it is used—God's love for people, our love for God, and our love for others.

Love has its origin in God; His very nature is love (1 John 4:8). He demonstrated this from the very beginning with Adam and Eve by allowing them to live after they had disobeyed Him. The love that God has for people continues through all generations, including this present age. And we can be certain that God's love will never change. This love is stated in an excellent way in John 3:16: "For God so loved the world that he gave his one and only Son that whoever believes in him shall not perish but have eternal life." It was God's love that resulted in Jesus's birth, death, and resurrection. Love is the very reason that Jesus came to earth—because

God loves us more than we can possibly imagine. Consider the following passages about God's love for us:

> But you, O Lord, are a God merciful and gracious, slow to anger and abounding in steadfast love and faithfulness. (Psalm 86:15)

> But God shows his love for us in that while we were still sinners, Christ died for us. (Romans 5:8)

> Beloved, let us love one another, for love is from God, and whoever loves has been born of God and knows God. Anyone who does not love does not know God, because God is love. (1 John 4:7–8)

> So we have come to know and to believe the love that God has for us. God is love, and whoever abides in love abides in God, and God abides in him. (1 John 4:16)

This is a small sample of passages that describe and affirm God's love for people. Notice in the last two verses it says, "God is love." He is a loving God who has demonstrated this throughout history. Why does God love people like you and me so much? It is not because we deserve this. It is because God's nature is to love. And God's love is a deep, deep love that knows no bounds. We know this because of the extensive evidence in the Bible and because of what we experience here on earth. It is because of God's love for us that we have an understanding of how to love others.

The second way love occurs is the love that people have for God; it is our response to God's love. In Deuteronomy 6:5, we find God's first commandment: "Love the Lord your God with all your heart and with all your soul and all your strength." God's desire is that we love Him. But not just to love Him as we love things or other people. He wants us to love Him wholeheartedly by putting Him first above all else. Why? It is because God desires a relationship with us—one that is based on love. If we put things or people ahead of God, we are putting our own interest or those of others ahead of Him. He requires that we put Him first—love God above all else. Remarkably, God desires a relationship with us, which is the most wonderful thing possible. Just imagine, the all-knowing, all-powerful, all-wise creator of the universe desires a personal relationship with you and me. He simply asks that we learn about Him (through the Bible and through His creation) and put our faith and trust in Him. How then can we demonstrate our love for God? It is by obeying His commandments and believing in Jesus, who was sent to us. This was made clear in the following two passages:

> If you love me, you will keep my commandments. (John 14:15)

> Whoever has my commandments and keeps them, it is he who loves me. And he who loves me will be loved by my Father, and I will love him and manifest myself to him. (John 14:21)

In response to a question, Jesus provided a wonderful summary of love in Matthew 22:36–40. "'Teacher, which is the great commandment in the Law?' And he said to him, 'You shall love the Lord your God with all your heart and with all your soul and with your entire mind.'" If we put things or people ahead of God, it interferes with our relationship with Him. God's expectation is that we put Him first, as stated in the first of the Ten Commandments. Anything short of this is disappointing to God.

The third way that love occurs is with people loving other people. In John 13:34, Jesus said, "A new command I give you: love one another. As I have loved you, so you must love one another." Note that He says, "You must love"! Love is not optional. Why was Jesus so insistent about this? Because He understands human nature; He knows that our natural tendency is to be selective in whom and how we love, or even to not love at all. Jesus took this one step further and made the shocking demand in Matthew 5:43–45: "You have heard that it was said, 'Love your neighbor and hate your enemy.' But I tell you, love your enemies and pray for those who persecute you, that you may be children of your Father in heaven."

We are to love even those who hate us and we consider our enemies (Luke 6:35). We must love! If we do not, the Bible warns that we are disobeying God (John 13:34). Therefore, we must love those who persecute us, those who disagree with us, those who have offended us, those who are different from us, those who are of a different race or nationality, those who are young or old, those who are rich or poor, those who are beautiful or homely, and those who are simply unlovable.

Obeying the command to love involves more than just saying the word. The Bible doesn't let us off that easily. It requires that we put our words into action. Biblical love involves doing. How do we know what love is or how to love? First John 3:16 states, "This is how we know what love is: Jesus Christ laid down his life for us. And we ought to lay down our lives for our brothers." Jesus demonstrated His love for us by His actions. He wants us to do the same by loving our neighbors as ourselves. Love is the very reason that Jesus came to earth—because He loves us more than we can possibly imagine. It is a deep love that knows no bounds.

How then do we put love into action with others? It is through helping, serving, showing kindness and mercy, listening, caring, and more. Jesus provided some examples in Matthew 25:36: "I needed clothes and you clothed me, I was sick and you looked after me, I was in prison and you came to visit me." These are all actions that demonstrate genuine love for our neighbors. Words alone are empty. In 1 John 2:5–6, we read, "But if anyone obeys his word, God's love is truly made complete in him. This is how we know we are in him: whoever claims to live in him must walk as Jesus did." We are to follow in the footsteps of Jesus. Matthew 22:36–40 says, "'Teacher, which is the great commandment in the Law?' And he said to him, 'You shall love the Lord your God with all your heart and with all your soul and with all your mind. This is the great and first commandment. And a second is like it: You shall love your neighbor as yourself. On these two commandments depend all the Law and the Prophets.'" Jesus is saying that by obeying the Ten Commandments (such as not lying or stealing), we are actually demonstrating love for our neighbors. We must intentionally demonstrate our love for others with everything we have—our heart, soul, and mind. The apostle Paul gave this excellent advice in 1 Corinthians 16:14: "Let all that you do be done in love."

In 1 Corinthians 13:4–7 (NIV), Paul describes love with sixteen characteristics. "Love is patient, love is kind. It does not envy, it does not boast, it is not proud. It does not dishonor others, it is not self-seeking, it is not easily angered, it keeps no record of wrongs. Love does not delight in evil but rejoices with the truth. It always protects, always trusts, always hopes, always perseveres." These can be categorized by what love is and what love is not. The type of love Paul is referring to here is agape, or love for one another, love that is based on God's love for us. These capture the essence of love.

What Love Is/Does	What Love Does Not Do / Is Not
patient	envy
kind	boast
always protects	proud
always trusts	keeps record of wrongs
never fails	delight in evil
always hopes	rude
always perseveres	self-seeking
rejoices with truth	easily angered

Paul prefaces this passage on love as "a most excellent way," and the words truly encompass excellence. As with forgiveness, none of these elements of love are particularly easy. It takes effort. In fact, some of these can be a great challenge for us. But that is what makes love so wonderful and what made the life and teachings of Jesus so unique. Everything He did and said was done out of love. When someone demonstrates genuine love, it stands out. People take notice. And so does God!

SERVING ONE ANOTHER

In ancient times, a servant was the equivalent to a slave, someone who did the biding of their master. They were bound to their owner and expected to be completely obedient. It was often a lowly position with little opportunity for change. They performed menial tasks, such as cleaning and cooking, but sometimes were given positions of responsibility. There is a second way the word *servant* is used in the Bible, which may come as a surprise; it was attributed to people at all levels in society, from laborers to kings. Individuals may have had positions of authority, yet they were deemed servants.

In Galatians 5:13, we are all called to serve one another—to literally be servants of one another. What does the Bible mean by this? Moses, Joshua, Abraham, Jacob, David, and Samuel were all called servants. They were servants of God, to be sure, but they were also servants of their peers and even those whom they led. They were both leaders and servants. They served in two ways. They served God, and they served others, no matter their social status. They served people in many ways, such as providing for, helping, protecting, and teaching.

The concept of a leader being a servant was made transparent by the ultimate servant, Jesus Christ. Jesus Himself described His purpose on earth as serving others. In Matthew 20:28, Jesus said, "For even the Son of Man came not to be served but to serve others and to give his life as a ransom for many" (NLT). Jesus, who is fully God, was born under the humblest of circumstances, for all people, thereby demonstrating true servanthood. He gave His all for us and became known as the suffering servant. Though a king, He served us in the fullest possible way. He provides salvation, helps us, protects us, and teaches us. In doing so, He shows us the perfect example of what it means to serve others—willingly, with humility, and with complete obedience.

In John chapter 13, Jesus provided a powerful example of what it means to serve others; He washed the feet of His disciples. That was a task for household servants or slaves, not a king. Why would Jesus do something so menial, so unbecoming of a leader? His purpose was to teach us a critically important lesson about what it means to follow Him. Our primary role is to serve others. Like Jesus, we are to do this willingly, with humility, and with complete obedience to God. Our task is to be obedient and do whatever He asks us to do. Even though we may have an important title or be in a great position of authority, Jesus wants us to remember that we are servants first.

The Bible provides guidance as to whom we should serve. We are to serve all those with whom we have contact, including family, friends, and neighbors. Jesus told a story about a man who had been robbed, beaten, and left for dead along a road. Two of his fellow countrymen passed by but found a reason to not help him. The next passerby was a foreigner but took pity on the man and attended to his needs. In this story, Jesus answered the question "Who is my neighbor?" It is whoever we encounter along life's roads. As the need arises, we may be called to people we do not know. We are to serve whoever God calls us to serve—at home, in our places of worship, in our community, or in distant lands.

The Bible does not specify how we should serve. Essentially, there are almost as many ways to serve as there are people in this world. We serve by seeking justice, helping, listening, teaching, fixing things, utilizing our spiritual gifts, giving our time, our money, or our talents, to name a few. Serving may include menial tasks, such as household chores, or tasks that require great skill or leadership. In Matthew 20:26, we read, "But whoever would be great among you must be your servant." And in 1 Peter 4:10, we read, "As each has received a gift, use it to serve one another, as good stewards of God's varied grace." The principle is that we evaluate the need and then see that it is filled. For many of us, this is more easily said than done. There are two important challenges when serving others. First, as Jesus taught, we must be humble enough to serve someone, and second, we must serve with genuine love. We may feel that the task of serving is beneath us and we cannot stoop to perform the service. Or perhaps some of those whom we are serving are not lovable or do not show appreciation. But if we cannot serve humbly and with love, we miss the point of serving.

Next to Jesus, one of the greatest examples of servant leadership in the Bible comes from the book of Nehemiah. Nehemiah lived during Israel's exile in the great city of Babylon. He ascended to the very important position of cup bearer for King Artaxerxes. A cup bearer was a position of authority and trust. One day, Nehemiah learned about the sad state of affairs in Jerusalem, where the walls and temple lay in ruin. With the king's blessing, Nehemiah traveled to Jerusalem on a mission to rebuild the broken-down walls and gates. In short, he overcame many obstacles and mobilized the entire city to accomplish the task. He accomplished all this with amazing speed—fifty-two days. Few, if any, of the laborers had ever done this kind of work before. Nehemiah did this because deeply wanted to bring honor to God and to protect the people of Jerusalem. He was the spiritual and physical leader of the people, but as importantly, he served the people in a profound way. He sought God's guidance, established a vision, genuinely cared for the people, built a team, maintained focus, and encouraged those around him. He did not seek power or recognition for himself but rather gave all the honor and glory to God. Credit is appropriately given here to Nehemiah. Often, we cannot see how God works in people's lives until we reflect on the past. Throughout his endeavors, it was evident that God's hand was with Nehemiah. After he sought God's wisdom and help, God responded by helping Nehemiah every step of the way. God works in amazing and subtle ways that are too wonderful for us to fully comprehend—when we commit to serving Him.

Thinking of ourselves as servants is not easy and does not come naturally, but the Bible teaches that it is important to serve others. There are several reasons why this is so. First, serving others is a way of showing love for them. In doing so, we are obeying Jesus's command to love others (John 13:34). Second, serving others makes use of the spiritual gifts that God has given us. Each person who has accepted Christ is given the Holy Spirit, and the Holy Spirit, in turn, gives spiritual gifts to them (1 Corinthians 12:8–11). The purpose of these gifts is to benefit others. Third, serving others brings glory to God. In 1 Peter 4:10–11, it says, "As each has received a gift, use it to serve one another, as good stewards of God's varied grace: whoever speaks, as one who speaks oracles of God; whoever serves, as one who serves by the strength that God supplies—in order that in everything God may be glorified through Jesus Christ." To Him belong glory and dominion forever and ever. When we show our love for others and utilize our God-given gifts and talents, it is pleasing to God. Fourth, serving results in a double blessing; both the giver and receiver are blessed.

How, when, and where should we serve others? The answer is simple— wherever the need is; at home, at work, at school, in neighborhoods, in communities, and more. When we have an attitude and lifestyle of service, we are able to see others the way Jesus does, with love and compassion. We serve Him because He served us and expects us to do the same. It is helpful to others and to us.

Printed in the United States
by Baker & Taylor Publisher Services